Monkey Bar Adventure

Monkey Bar Adventure

Product of "Ministry from the Monkey Bars"

Angela L. Kirkpatrick

iUniverse, Inc.
New York Lincoln Shanghai

Monkey Bar Adventure
Product of "Ministry from the Monkey Bars"

iUniverse books may be ordered through booksellers or by contacting:

iUniverse
2021 Pine Lake Road, Suite 100
Lincoln, NE 68512
www.iuniverse.com
1-800-Authors (1-800-288-4677)

ISBN-13: 978-0-595-35624-9 (pbk)
ISBN-13: 978-0-595-80102-2 (ebk)
ISBN-10: 0-595-35624-9 (pbk)
ISBN-10: 0-595-80102-1 (ebk)

Printed in the United States of America

Mark 10:14–16

He said to them "Let the children come to me, and do not hinder them, for the kingdom of God belongs to such as these. I tell you the truth, anyone who will not receive the kingdom of God like a little child will never enter it." And he took the children in his arms and, put his hands on them and blessed them. (NIV)

"Take your time with God as seriously as you want your children to take their time with you."

Dedicated to: Kaylyn and Camper
You are my joy and my teachers.
I love you both.

ACKNOWLEDGMENTS

Rick,

You are God's gift to me this side of heaven. I love you and thank you for being the perfect man for me. You are in my heart and my soul from now to eternity.

Kaylyn,

My princess, you amaze me every day. Someday you will know the depth and breadth of the impact you have on my life. You have created in me a desire to serve my Father in heaven in a way that will cause Him to say, "Well done good and faithful servant."

Camper,

My son, you are the light of my life. I look at you and wonder each day what Jesus must have been like as a child. You inspire me to look at all children through the eyes of Christ.

Mom,

Thank you for the light you shine. You raise me up, you help me press on, and I thank you now for giving to the Lord. You are my rock, my sanctuary, and my arms of love. I love you.

My family,

Thank you for your support, encouragement, and unconditional love. God continues to use each of you to bring me out of darkness and into His light. You are my life team and it is in each of you that I see the face of God on a daily basis. I love you!

Sweet Katy,

Thank you for being a precious child of God who gently and lovingly makes a difference in the lives of everyone you meet.

Precious Josiah,

Thank you for being a *faith giant* by which many of us are unable to measure up. Sing loud with all the praise that heaven contains. I treasure the idea that I will meet you at the throne of grace.

Sharon Cecil,

Thank you for hearing my heart and seeing my vision. You created a master piece in moments and captured the essence of *Monkey Bar Adventure*.

Stephen and Karen,

Under the gravest of earthly circumstances, God worked through you to bring my family into the loving arms of a church family that would not let go. You are precious to me and I will forever treasure the lessons learned, the blessings bestowed, and the gifts discovered.

Family at Grace,

Your open hearts and doors have encouraged me to walk daily in God's light. Many of you have eternally impacted my life with hugs, tears (big bladders behind our eyes), laughter (even the silent or uncontrollable kind), opportunities, editing, fellowship, and friendship. I love each of you as brothers and sisters in Christ.

FOREWORD

Monkey Bar Adventure is a delightful book filled with lots of "spiritual meat." The pages of this book contain a wonderful glimpse into the life of a godly, loving mother and her two delightful children. As a person who is ever vigilant for ways God is speaking to her, Angela has often discovered his voice in and through the words and actions of her children. The following pages contain "parables" that reveal many spiritual truths to the reader. I know for a fact that this book is a gift of God to Angela, a gift that she wants to share with the world. You will empathize, sympathize, laugh, cry, and rejoice with the characters in *Monkey Bar Adventure.*

As her pastor, I have watched Angela blossom into a wonderful, faithful, obedient child of God. Her greatest desire is to serve God to the best of her ability. She feels that God has richly blessed her life and she desires to be a blessing to others. This book is her effort to do just that.

Stephen Schmidt; Pastor
Grace United Methodist Church
Copperas Cove, Texas

PREFACE

I am so thrilled to be sharing this with you. I am Angela Kirkpatrick. I live in Copperas Cove, Texas, and have spent most of my life here. I grew up in faith but my true spiritual journey began in January 2003. A good friend of mine, Jean, was truly frightened by having to go back because of an abnormal test from the doctor. She was horrified by the possibility of cancer and was physically shaken. As she sat on my couch at work crying in fear I knelt down and asked her if I could pray with her. I had never done that and I was so afraid myself. I do not remember what I said and I do not think it mattered. We both cried and then we talked. I gave her my Pastor's phone number and that concluded our meeting. A day or so later she went to see him and you would not believe what he said. He actually told her that if she had any questions she was to first ask me. He then instructed her that she was to read her Bible for five minutes a day and to pray for one minute a day. He also said that I was supposed to do that with her. I nearly fell off my chair and responded, "What? Ask me? Are you serious?" I then said, "Okay, but let me clarify that we may spend lots of time going back to Stephen [the pastor]. I have not exactly been studying my Bible as much as I should either."

From that day on we met each morning and held each other accountable to that "5:1" challenge. The amazing thing was that five minutes turned into fifteen minutes of reading, and one minute of praying became ten minutes. We talked and we prayed through situations that caused us pain. We sought guidance before overreacting and held each other accountable to being thankful for the many blessings that we were experiencing at that time. Jean is probably my closest spiritual confidant, and I owe Stephen an eternal "thank you" for challenging us to spend six minutes a day with God. Six minutes! Six minutes changed my life and I did not even know it was happening. From that six minutes came *Steps to Faith, Ministry from the Monkey Bars,* and *Monkey Bar Adventure.* I challenge each of you to find a friend and try that "5:1" challenge for one month. You cannot imagine the blessings that you will reap from time with your Father.

As a high school teacher I have had the privilege of teaching some really wonderful high school students. I am currently teaching science, and I love my job! That is also an amazing story of God's mighty hand working in my life that I hope to someday share. I have taught leadership and service learning classes in the past, where I would begin a time management unit by asking my students to write down a daily schedule. I found that they were spending only a few minutes of time per day, if any, with their parents and families. I was devastated for them. I am thankful that my children are still young and enter the car or house every day just dying to tell me what happened during the day. When I think of the difference that a few minutes of time can actually make, I feel sad that I spent so many years depriving my Heavenly Father of that same joy. Take your time with God as seriously as you want your children to take their time with you.

Included in this book is a series of stories, many of which are situations that have occurred in houses all over the world and that have made parents laugh, cry, scream, and be thankful. God is a very persistent parent and has been patient with me about this project. If you are reading it, it is because God's mighty hand took a strong hold of my pride and dragged it kicking and screaming out of my heart. I pray for my children, as the subjects of this book. I pray for you as you read this book. I pray that you will look at the children in your life, see what Jesus sees in them, and be blessed in all of the moments you have with them. Come with me and together we will experience a *Monkey Bar Adventure* as we inherit the kingdom of heaven.

CONTENTS

Perfect Parent—Perfect Child of God

Do you plan to have children? Are you already a parent? Perhaps you are a grandparent. Are you a teacher? Do you deal with children on a regular basis? Well, I learned quickly that I could have been a perfect parent had God seen fit to send me perfect children, right???

With that said, I would like to do an activity with you.

I would like you to make a list of things that a perfect child would and would not do.

A Perfect Child Would…	A Perfect Child Would Not…
1.	1.
2.	2.
3.	3.
4.	4.
5.	5.
6.	6.
7.	7.
8.	8.
9.	9.
10.	10.
11.	11.
12.	12.
13.	13.
14.	14.
15	15.

I will give you a couple of mine to get us started. My perfect child *would* tell me every day that she/he loves me. My perfect child *would not* throw another fit in church or anywhere else!

Do not move on in your reading until you do this activity. It will help you go through the rest of the stories with deeper insight. If you are of the mindset that writing in books is a bad idea, use a scrap piece of paper, but I want you to stop right now and do this. Have some fun. Most of our children have, at times, either made us so mad we thought our head might explode or so proud we might just burst. Let us start by compiling a list of characteristics of that perfect child. Think of all the times they have made you smile or cry with pride. Write them down, and don't stop until you have covered at least fifteen perfect moments! Now look at those behaviors that make you crazy, angry, or embarrassed. I would be surprised if you were not able to come up with at least ten examples of behaviors that you would like to change!

Do not move on in this book until you are satisfied with your list.

Next to the top line of each column following the words "A Perfect Child," add the words "of God." How does your list look now? That experience is what Stephen Covey calls a paradigm shift. It is this paradigm that gave birth to *Monkey Bar Adventure*.

I have learned through my little angels that God, my Father, has a great sense of humor. As I grow in my relationship with Him, my children have taught me more about "godly parenting" than I could have ever imagined. I also know that Jesus must have had some great gut laughs at my expense because of the promise in

Galatians 6:7

"Do not be deceived: God cannot be mocked. A man reaps what he sows." (NIV)

and the curse from your mother, when she said, "I hope you have one just like you!"

Think about that for just one minute. From the time of the fall, our children would be as much a blessing as a curse, and mothers have taken comfort in that for generations. The reverse is also true; as it says in

1 John 3:1

How great is the love the Father has lavished on us, that we should be called children of God! And that is what we are! The reason the world does not know us is that it did not know Him. (NIV)

2 Corinthians 6:18

I will be your Father, and you will be my sons and daughters, declares the Lord almighty. (NIV)

Perfect parents are first children of God!

In order for each of us to come anywhere near being an adequate parent we must first work toward becoming a perfect child—of God! God is my Father. He loves me more than I will ever love my children and that is hard to conceptualize. I am His child and I have found that I am not nearly as grown up as I thought I was. I act childish in far too many instances, and in others, I know He longs for the days when I was childlike in my faith. God blessed me with two children who have taught me a great deal about being a good parent and a great child of God! Sound funny? Well, I hope that the lessons I have learned help you to look at the way your children make you feel, even in their terrible moments, and see that we often make our Heavenly Father feel the exact same way. I hope you see in them what Jesus saw, when He said in

Matthew 19:14

"Let the children come to me. Don't stop them! For the kingdom of heaven belongs to such as these." (NIV)

The following song lyrics were written during this journey, and in them you will find many of the stories and lessons being shared throughout the book. As you read I encourage you to reflect on those moments when your children have had "monster moments," "monkey moments," and "angel moments." Look into their hearts and see that they truly are made for "fun and games," and yet we will have many opportunities to ask "Who is teaching whom?" Take comfort in knowing that in those "911 Parenting Moments" God is with us and He understands because He has gone through all of those moments with each of us.

Monkey Bar Adventure

Written by: Angela Kirkpatrick
For: Ministry from the Monkey Bars
Dedicated to my little angels: Kaylyn and Camper

It's a Monkey Bar adventure that we're going on.
We'll laugh, we'll play, we'll learn, we'll pray and carry on.
And as our children teach us we will come to know.
Our Father up in Heaven loves us so.

Sometimes they're monsters…Sometimes they're monkeys…
Sometimes they're little angels without wings.
But we will learn that's why Jesus loves them.
They learn, they reach, they love, they ask, they sing.

It's a Monkey Bar adventure that we're going to see.
We'll laugh, we'll play, we'll learn, we'll pray and we will be,
Content to see a smile on every child's face,
And learn about God's love and Jesus' grace.

Sometimes they're monsters…Sometimes they're monkeys…
Sometimes they're little angels without wings.
But we will learn that's why Jesus loves them.
They learn, they reach, they love, they ask, they sing.

It's a Monkey Bar adventure that will help us grow.
We'll laugh, we'll play, we'll learn, we'll pray and we will go,
Out into a world that needs to know His love,
And teach of grace and mercy from above.

Sometimes they're monsters…Sometimes they're monkeys…
Sometimes they're little angels without wings.
But we will learn that's why Jesus loves them.
They learn, they reach, they love, they ask, they sing.

Kaylyn and Camper—I love you!

MONSTER MOMENTS

Monster moments are those times when we feel like screaming. They come and go, and it is in these moments that other parents can empathize with our plight. Sometimes our children seem to have one primary goal for the day and that is to drive us crazy. In this section we will look at those moments from God's perspective. We will reflect on our own monster moments and laugh a little at the childlike behaviors that contribute to them. Children want answers! They need protection, and they are extremely protective. They ask, and ask, and ask! They focus completely, also known as nagging, and are passionate about life. Children make impressions, some of which are good and some which are not. Finally, children reflect perfection. It is sometimes an internal reflection, but in them we can see Jesus. As you read and recall the "monster moments," remember that God as our Father has had to endure generation after generation of monster behavior from His children.

"But *Why?*"—"Because I Said So!"—Children Want Answers
Half-Hearted Effort—Children Need Correction
"He Messed Up My Castle"—Children Are Protective
Manners 101—Children *Ask!*
One-Track Mind—Children Focus Completely
Texas-Sized Tantrum—Children Are Passionate!
What Child Are You Describing?—Children Make Impressions
What Have You Done?—Children Reflect Perfection

"But *Why?*"—"Because I Said So!" Children Want Answers

Ephesians 6:1–4

Children obey your parents in the Lord, for this is right. "Honor your father and mother"—which is the first commandment with a promise— "that it may go well with you and that you may enjoy long life on the earth." Fathers, do not exasperate your children; instead, bring them up in the training and instruction of the Lord. (NIV)

Did you ever swear as a child that you would never use the sentence, "Because I said so!"? I hated that answer as a child and as a teenager. How many of you have already broken that vow? My sweet daughter was a very persistent, inquisitive, and verbal two-year-old. She often frightened and amazed us with the language she used and "Why?" was a very early question. She also did not sleep well, or for very long, so at that point I was working on a two-year sleep deprivation cycle. I felt like Kaylyn was the only child on the planet who always needed to know *why* she had to go to bed, *why* she couldn't play in the street, *why* I would not read to her right then, *why* she could not paint in the living room, *why* lipstick does not come out of the carpet, *why* she could not put the baby lotion on herself, *why* she had to have a shot, *why* she couldn't have everything she wanted…*why? Why? Why?* Grrr! "Because I said so!" We say it because they continue to ask if they are not satisfied with the answer. We say it because we are tired of hearing the question. We say it because we actually can't answer the question. We say it because shouldn't our vast life experiences be reason enough?!

How many of us have ever asked God, "*Whhhyyyy?*"

Why do I have to work with her?
Why do swim lessons cost so much?
Why can't they manage their money better?
Why don't people give at church?
Why doesn't my husband know what I am thinking?
Why can't I get that job?
Why does she have it all?
Why don't they see my side of the story?
Why is he like that?
Why doesn't God give me what I want?

Why do I have to go through this?
Why can't my kids act right in church?
Why does my spouse have to go to war?
Why do the good people have to die?
Why do children die and *why* is that fair?
Why? *Why*? *Why*?

Imagine that sound one million people over!

Does God say "Because I said so!"? Maybe not in so many words, but after a million whiny complaints I would imagine He has felt like it a time or two. God answers our prayers and has given us perfect guidelines. God desires consistent (persistent) contact with Him. God wants us to know but God wants us to read and learn. God wants us to know enough to answer our children biblically and he has provided us with several stock answers to many of those questions. My favorite is the commandment in Ephesians 6:1–4.

How cool is that? It is a perfect biblical reason to listen to your parents, but remember the last instruction: "Fathers, do not exasperate your children; instead, bring them up in the training and instruction of the Lord." Before saying "Because I said so!" recall for a moment if that would have been an exasperating answer for you to hear as a child. My dear friend in Christ, remember God will never turn His back on us when we are talking to Him. He will listen and always do what is right for us. Can we say the same for ourselves in regard to our children? When they ask why, ask yourself, "What might Jesus say?" If you do not know, either look it up or simply look up! The funny irony here is that our Father in heaven knew we would continue to whine and ask why, and He blessed us with children who would be a constant reminder that "*Why*?" can be just as irritating as "Because I said so!"

Can you think of ways that you might be exasperating your children? If so, confess them and ask God to help you learn from this point forward to work toward bringing them up in the training and instruction of the Lord.

_____

_____

_____

_____

_____

_____

_____

Jesus loves children because they want answers. Jesus loves you.

Half-Hearted Effort
Children Need Correction

Revelation 3:15–16

I know your deeds, that you are neither cold nor hot. I wish you were either one or the other! So, because you are lukewarm—neither hot nor cold—I am about to spit you out of my mouth. (NIV)

Ephesians 6:7

Serve wholeheartedly, as if you were serving the Lord, not men. (NIV)

Kaylyn had been in first grade for about one month. She had been doing very well, and we were very excited to see the amazing light that seemed to be coming on. Mrs. Wade, thank you! She came home with a graded assignment for which she was supposed to have found words in the newspaper that started with each letter of the alphabet. She had only done seventeen letters and received a poor grade. This was not something that she should have had trouble with, and daddy and I pretty much let her have it. It was unacceptable because she had not done her best. It was disappointing because she was blaming her classmates for distracting her. We were angry because she did not seem to be bothered by this mediocrity that was out of character for her. We were going to make it clear that we never expected to see a grade like that again on something she should have aced. I am not proud of it, but we did bring her to tears, and she completely redid the assignment. At six years old we were facing her first "half-hearted effort" and we blasted her for it.

The real kicker is God placed on my heart those scriptures from Revelation and Ephesians.

I had to wonder. How many times had I put forth that half-hearted, lukewarm, mediocre, effort and left just glad to be done with the assignment. Had I done that in school? Had I done that in my home? Had I done that in my relationships with my family? Had I done that with God? God wants me to be on fire for Him, not cold, not warm, but flaming hot and unable to contain my fervor for Him. Had I ever splashed cold water on someone else who was on fire?

Take a minute and confess some of those times when you have fallen short of
your best effort.

_____
_____
_____
_____
_____
_____
_____
_____

As the questions flooded my mind, I found myself begging forgiveness and
becoming more determined to focus on my fire first. Correct me Lord!

Jesus loves children because they need correction. Jesus loves you.

"He Messed Up My Castle"
Children Are Protective

Psalm 145:13

Your kingdom is an everlasting kingdom, and your dominion endures through all generations. The Lord is faithful to all his promises and loving toward all he has made. (NIV)

"Mommy, Camper stepped on my castle. He broke it, and I worked really hard on it!" She begins to cry.

"No I dinit! Kaywyn didit!" my son pipes in to defend himself, and yes, he is telling a bold-faced lie.

The following was my thought process on how to handle the situation:

1. Tell her not to build where he can destroy it (knowing he just wants to play with her).
2. Yell/Tell him that that is not nice (knowing she wants him to be in trouble).
3. Ignore them and/or tell them to handle it (knowing that someone will get hit).
4. Ask her what she wants me to do about it (knowing that answer would be to spank him, beat him, ground him, and never feed him again)
5. Tell her to beat him to the punch and destroy it herself (That is my sister's pat answer).
6. Here we go. Help her rebuild her castle and teach her to share or give him a job to help. Yep, that is the one. Okay, out of my head and into action.

It worked and we had a nice time playing together for about thirty minutes. Then at the end we had to "destroy" it anyway to put it away, but this time it was fun and both kids were laughing.

Teaching children to get along, to be nice to their sibling's creations, and to clean up after themselves, all strike me as funny when I try to think from God's perspective. God must often look down and be frustrated at what we have done to His creation. We know that the great flood and Noah's Ark were a prime example of Him using tactic #5. There have been times when Kaylyn has knocked down her own creation just to make sure her brother or cousin did not do it first. Another biblical example is Moses leading the Israelites across the Red Sea; we learn of the God who used #1—Go where they cannot follow. God handing down the Ten Commandments in Exodus, using #2—Yell/Telling the Israelites to be nice…knowing that they deserved to be punished. Job is a sad example of God using #3—Ignoring him, and letting Job handle it (knowing Job would get hit). Revelation is the culmination of God our Father saying to His Son Jesus, our brother in God's family, "That *is it!* I have had enough!," and using #6— "Together My Son we will build your kingdom that cannot be destroyed and over which You will reign for eternity. Your brothers and sisters will have a new and perfect job…praise and worship! It will be a kingdom where Satan's evil arm can no longer reach!"—AMEN

Teach your children to be protective of their relationships with God, family, and their future families.

Jesus loves children because they are protective. Jesus loves you.

Manners 101
Children *Ask*!

Luke 11:9

"So I say to you: Ask and it will be given to you, seek and you will find, knock and the door will be opened." (NIV)

I am standing in my kitchen, not that I spend much time there, and I hear the familiar whining of my two-year-old son. Picture for a moment your two-year-old. Two-year-olds are without a doubt the most beautiful creations on the planet, and my son is no exception. I look down at this beautiful tiny miracle and grimace at the sound coming from his mouth. It is an ugly, broken-door-in-a-haunted-house sort of whine. "Piinnngguull, I waannnaa Piinnngggguuulll!" This is, of course, the eighth time he has said this.

I stand there, looking at him, shift my weight to one side, place my hand on my hip and wait.

He repeats himself, this time with a foot stomp, "Iyanna Piiinnnngggguuulle."

I raise one eyebrow, hoping to communicate my message, because I desperately want to give him what he wants.

Do we love to give our kids what they want and make them happy?

So what am I waiting for? That's right…the magic word.

Sometimes this results in a standoff but not today. It dawns on him what I am waiting for, and here it comes, in a lot sweeter voice, "Pingull pweeze."

I now get to be the hero, all is forgiven for torturing him, and I hand him one Pringle. I wait…he smiles and with an entire Pringle in his mouth he says, "Danku!"

Ta da!

Why do we go through this ritual?

To teach patience,
To teach manners,
To teach being appreciative (of one potato chip),
To teach them to read body language we hope will work in public,
To teach them to ask for what they want,
To teach them to ask nicely,
and to say thank you immediately.

How many times a day do we say please and thank you to our Heavenly Father (who by the way is trying to teach us the same list)? I picture God, hand on His hip, eyebrow raised, looking at me...I am whining, complaining, demanding, begging for something, when finally, in my deepest desperation, I cry out..."Pleeaasssee!" and you know what He handed me?—Jesus.

Thank You!

What were some of the manners that you learned from your parents and grandparents?

_____

_____

_____

_____

_____

_____

_____

Philippians 4:6

Do not be anxious about anything, but in everything, by prayer and petition, with thanksgiving, present your requests to God. (NIV)

Do not be anxious (demanding or impatient) about anything, but in everything, by prayer and petition (ask, and ask nicely), with thanksgiving (always say thank you), present your requests to God (ask your Father, and remember your manners).

Jesus loves them because they *ask*! Jesus loves you!

One-Track Mind
Children Focus Completely

Deuteronomy 6:5–7

Love the Lord your God with all your heart and with all your soul and with all your strength. These commandments that I give you today are to be upon your hearts. Impress them on your children. Talk about them when you sit at home and when you walk along the road, when you lie down, and when you get up. (NIV)

Have your children ever gotten a thought or song stuck in their heads? (*The Wheels on the Bus* perhaps?) I learned very early that I absolutely could not tell my two-year-old daughter what we might be doing the upcoming weekend. There are two problems with telling children good news in advance: 1) they will ask and be relentless in their questions, and 2) You could accidentally tell a lie, which to a child like Kaylyn is devastating.

Take a minute and think about the following situations:

1. Children in the car on a trip to grandma's house.
2. Telling your children on Monday that you will go to McDonald's on Friday.
3. Discussing a child's birthday party in March when the date is in May.
4. Your house in November, when every TV commercial is about Christmas toys.
5. Your child's teacher tells them two weeks in advance about a field trip to the zoo.
6. Your child's favorite song to sing…over and over and over again.
7. The book you must have read 1,000 times.

I believe God enjoys the relentless persistence of kids. I also believe that it is our job to get them "stuck" on a movie/message/song about God. Our job as parents is not to squelch the persistent passion that children have for new things, or the same things, but to learn from it, to remember what it feels like to love something so much or to want something so much that we just might burst.

What things happen to us as we grow up that squelch our passion?

_____

_____

_____

_____

_____

_____

_____

Pray that you are able to let go of those feelings and invite the Spirit into your heart and to reignite your passion for a Savior who died a horrific death just for you.

Jesus loves children because they focus completely. Jesus loves you.

Texas-Sized Tantrum
Children Are Passionate!

<u>Ephesians 4:31</u>

Get rid of all bitterness, rage and anger, brawling and slander, along with every form of malice. (NIV)

My sweet son is two, and he seems to be the typical example of a two-year-old. He is sweet, funny, curious, and learns new things every moment of every day. When he speaks, I smile. His hugs are the most awesome part of my day because he still hugs back and he still fits perfectly on my shoulder. But, he also has, on several occasions, thrown those patented two-year-old tantrums…head thrown back, mouth wide open, screaming, and, if I happen to be holding his hand, he will drop like a hooked fish flopping around. He becomes dead weight and is no longer able to remember how to stand on his own two legs. My desired response is to have a Texas-sized overreaction to this and to match scene for scene his behavior. I would like to say that I learned not to actually do that before I became a parent, but I have to confess that I did match my daughter one time. It did not have the desired outcome, and my husband had to step in. Thank you for my husband…I think Kaylyn owes her life to him.

How did you respond the first time your child threw a tantrum?

_____

_____

_____

_____

_____

_____

_____

I have learned to remove my son from the situation and give him a chance to calm down. I do not leave him, even though when this happens in public I would really like to pretend he is not mine. I have also learned the hard way that physical restraint might make me feel like I am the big strong parent as I grit my teeth to hold him, but it only causes him to raise the decibel level to somewhere near window shattering. It is at these moments of parenting when I find myself wondering if God is actually laughing. I am convinced He has a sense of humor. Why else would He give two strong-willed parents two stronger-willed children other than to laugh and teach us a lesson or two.

Picture our Father in heaven walking with us on life's journey. We decide that the way is too difficult. He takes hold of our hands and reassures us that His will is perfect and that He knows best. (Have you ever wished that your kids would just trust that you know best!?) We, in our shortsightedness, protest, "Father, I can't go through that. I don't want to go to the doctor. I just can't get through to my kids. I don't think I can do that job. I cannot stand that person. Why is everyone against me? But I want the car now!" We, at this point, are literally kicking our spiritual feet out from under us, dropping to the floor, and crying or pouting that life is not fair! God in His wisdom will bring us to a quiet place and wait patiently for us to figure out that He is right...or that we are not going to get our way right now.

We, just like our children, cannot see past the immediate to the greater purpose. My Father's purpose for my life is far greater than I can imagine, and every move I make in life is either both quiet listening and obeying or it is, "Do it my way...and pay the consequence!" God does not desire for us to be apart from Him. He desires to help us, uphold us, teach us, love us, strengthen us, and help us grow. Sometimes we have to stop trying to yank our Father's shoulder out of the socket and be comforted by that strong hand that guides us through this life on earth. Praise our Father who does not hold us down. He does not turn His back on us, and He does not deny us. He waits for us to get ourselves together while He pains for us because we make everything harder than it needs to be. Most importantly, He forgives us when we embarrass Him.

Heavenly Father,

Regardless of my past and my present, I look to You for a future that is bright and promising as a member of Your family. Father, I want to get rid of those feelings that I harbor toward people who have hurt me. I want all bitterness, rage, and anger to be flushed from my heart so that You may come in and abide with me. Help me control my tongue, and keep slander and malice out of my head so that I am not tempted to say it. Lord, only You can heal the wounds that are deeply rooted in my heart and being fertilized by those constant negative emotions. I love You, and I need You to help me let go and forgive. Help me be passionate and not burdened.

In Jesus' Name,

Me

Jesus loves children because they are passionate. Jesus loves you.

What Child Are You Describing?
Children Make Impressions

1 Timothy 3:4

He must manage his own family well and see that his children obey him with the proper respect. (NIV)

Ephesians 6:1

Children obey your parents in the Lord, for this is right. (NIV)

It is Sunday morning, any Sunday morning in the fall of 2001 or spring of 2002. I have a new son and a three-and-a half-year-old daughter. I get up...good so far, right? I am trying to get ready for church, when all of a sudden my children become demon possessed. They are crying and not cooperating during the few moments we have to get dressed. My son has just thrown up on his clothes. My daughter does not want to brush her teeth. I cannot find one of her shoes (and there is no other option because she has just had a growth spurt today!). My son decides that he needs to nurse again to replace the food he just puked all over himself. Kaylyn does not want cereal and spills her juice on the floor. Camper poops while I am feeding him, and Kaylyn now needs me to wipe her bottom as she too had to go "poopie" two minutes after we should have already pulled out of the driveway. Rick would have helped but he really had no idea it was going on, and I much preferred to just be irritated and grumpy rather than to humble myself and ask for help.

We arrive at church frazzled, frustrated, and fully expecting credit from God that we even made it to church. I reach up to discover that I only have one earring on, and I realize that I have mascara on only one eye. Suddenly, one of the ladies in church said to Kaylyn, "That is a very pretty dress."

My demon-possessed daughter almost curtseys and replies "Thank you very much."

Both my husband and I looked in amazement at her response. The lady then said, "Your children are so sweet and well mannered."

We say, "Thank you," and chuckle to ourselves. We are thankful that our children behave in public. They do put their best foot forward...hmmm! My Father in heaven might also want me to complain only in the privacy of my prayers so that I, too, can put my best foot forward with my family, my job, my ministry, and so on.

Raise them right! Our children will obey us as well as we obey Him!

Take a moment and recall a time when you probably did not put your best foot forward. Ask God to help you prepare so that the next time an opportunity comes your way to make an impression for Christ you will be ready. Can you think of a time when someone made a poor impression on you? Write a prayer for that person, and then write one for yourself that you are willing to forgive and forget, as God does, that impression and start fresh.

_____

_____

_____

_____

_____

_____

_____

_____

_____

_____

_____

_____

_____

_____

_____

_____

_____

_____

_____

_____

_____

_____

Jesus loves children because they make impressions. Jesus loves you.

What Have You Done?
Children Reflect Perfection

<u>Genesis 1:27</u>

So God created man in his own image, in the image of God he created him; male and female he created them. (NIV)

<u>Genesis 3:13</u>

Then the LORD God said to the woman, "What is this you have done?" The woman said, "The serpent deceived me, and I ate." (NIV)

In January 2005 Camper was three years old and at Mimi's house. When Rick came in he hugged Camper and found what he thought was cat hair on Camper's shirt. Rick left the room, and Mimi walked over to the counter, where Camper was sitting surrounded by his art supplies. She looked at the counter, and lo and behold, it was covered with hair. The realization of what had occurred hit her.

She looked at Camper, knowing that he had taken several swipes at the front of his hair, and asked (in a slightly, *Oh my gosh, he did this at my house!!* tone of voice) "What did you do?"

Camper gave his standard (lips puckered, eyes drooping, puddles forming, I don't know how that happened) look.

Thank goodness he is a boy. We took him down to Bubba, who gave him his first burr cut…actually it was really cute.

Picture your child coming into the living room having just cut the front of his hair a quarter of an inch from his scalp. The typical parent overreaction happens, "What have you done?"

The child, who was proud, is now on the verge of tears and asks, "Do you still love me?"

How heartbreaking. "Of course I love you," as the parent is now feeling guilty for overreacting.

We, as parents, cannot always control our reactions. Jesus never winced at the sight of the lepers or judged with his expression those who were possessed. Jesus never turned away from sinners, and he never shrieked at the bad things people did. The funny thing is that in today's superficial society, a bad haircut can feel like leprosy.

Why is it that we cannot always control our immediate reactions?

_____

_____

_____

_____

_____

_____

_____

When our children cut their hair early in life—or perhaps when they dye their hair or pierce their nose as teenagers—we wish desperately for the ability to say, "Grow! Be long! Be healed! Be through with this 'phase'! Be responsible for your own actions!"

I wonder, does our loving Father in heaven look at each of us in our society of hair dye, perms, make-up, cosmetic surgery, tummy tucks, overindulgence, and revealing clothes and say "My child, what have you done? You are in my image…surely you do not believe that what you have done looks better that my original creation? My child, you must not blame others for your actions. I love you, and you are perfect just as I made you!"

We are made in His image. Be convicted to reflect that image every day. Do people look at you and see God or Jesus?

_____

_____

_____

_____

_____

_____

_____

Jesus loves children because they reflect perfection. Jesus loves you.

MONKEY MOMENTS

Monkey moments are those moments in life when you find yourself less angry and more amazed at what your children do or are able to accomplish in the right circumstances. Children are monkeys by nature. Children are curious about everything. They seek solutions and believe they can do it. Children trust. They practice new skills and they are not ashamed. They wonder and are wonderful. A child can see things in this world that an adult has long missed. As you read through this section, recall those moments when your children made you laugh because they saw the world from that sweet childlike perspective.

Childproof or Adultproof?
Children Are Curious

Psalm 116:6

The LORD protects the simple hearted; when I was in great need, he saved me. (NIV)

Do you know children who seem to have a multitude of angels assigned to their protection? My niece Raegan is one of those children. When she was eighteen months old, she was at my house one evening. We were in the bathroom so that all three children, her and my two, could take a bath. The bath went fine and I was feeling really proud of myself for successfully bathing all three children. I got her out first, dried her off, and put her diaper on. I reached to remove my two-year-old son, and in the instant that it took she had opened the cupboard, pulled out the bleach toilet cleaner with the childproof cap, got the cap off, and raised the bottle toward her mouth! My reaction was swift…"Noooo!" (I screamed with a volume that shook the window and scared both of my kids.) I snatched the cleaner with the right hand, popped her head with my left hand (not sure why I did that??), slammed the cleaner on the counter, and thumped her hand! She looked at me…not with fear, not with tears, but with pure "What is wrong with you?" and, if she had had eyebrows, one of them was definitely raised. The entire exchange took less than ten seconds.

Now, the funny part of this scenario was that all I could think was, "There is no way you are going to drink bleach on my clock!" How utterly stupid…as if anyone would say, oh nice, go ahead. I also was afraid for my sister who had to, on a daily basis, deal with a child who is smart, quick, and curious. Raegan was a master locksmith from the moment she could walk, and there is no such thing as childproof for her. She is very skilled, but when you mix skills like that with inexperience you get danger! She, in spite of my one-second neglect, had angels watching over her, and I take great comfort in the promise in Psalm 116:6 that He will protect and save her from her Aunt.

My Father in heaven childproofs things for me. There are times when a task is easy for me and hard for someone else and vice versa. Picture for a moment the infamous pickle jar. Who can open it with the least effort? It is not always the strongest person but often a feeble grandma who knows the secret to pop the lid. When we act in God's will, we will find that tasks become much easier. God's timing for our life is a crucial factor, and when we get in a hurry we find the antagonist to peace. Those people who know the secret of God's timing are those who have learned that an intricate balance exists between peace that comes in the waiting and an active childlike curiosity. God protects the simple hearted, and He taught me that He was protecting Raegan. I believe her curiosity will eventually become an unquenchable thirst to learn. What greater gift is there for a child of God? I do laugh, knowing that there will be a time when Raegan will wish that she did not know how to open the toilet cleaner, or how to use it. Until that time, I will probably continue to overreact to her dangerous curiosity and thank God when He protects her for me.

Are there things around you that frighten you? What are the irrational fears that we have that we seem to impose on our children?

_____

_____

_____

_____

_____

_____

_____

Have you lost some of that childlike curiosity that God might be able to use?

_____

_____

_____

_____

_____

_____

Jesus loves children because they are curious. Jesus loves you!

Creative Problem Solving
Children Seek Solutions

Galatians 6:2

Carry each other's burdens, and in this way you will fulfill the law of Christ. (NIV)

My two-and-a-half-year-old son demonstrated his creative problem solving when trying to figure out what to do with a runny nose. Now, what would you do? Get a tissue from your purse? Grab a hanky from your pocket? Borrow a tissue from a friend or family member? Perhaps you might even go to the restroom to use some toilet paper? Worse case scenario…you might snuff it up or use your shirt? Well, my precious (and I mean precious) son found an alternative…very creative and slightly disgusting solution to his nose running dilemma. He first proclaimed, "My nose is running!" Then, before anyone could respond, he dropped to the floor and proceeded to wipe his nose in one big right-to-left motion across Mimi's usually clean carpet. My husband and I laughed hysterically, and my son looked at us as if to say, "Well what did you expect me to do?" Once again, I am certain that my Father in heaven chuckled at a child's ability to solve a problem in a most unusual way. I also believe God sometimes is creative in helping us solve our problems. God is a faithful Father who, when we are unable to think of a solution, or just are not listening to Him, has an amazing way of dropping just the right person into our life to provide that answer. In Galatians we are told to carry each other's burdens.

For me, this is a biblical way of reminding us that two heads are better than one. God did design us for fellowship in times of joy and in times of problems. Just don't be alarmed by those times when we just might have to drop to our knees on the floor, put all pride aside, and see how simple the solution actually is. Oh yes…and so what if someone laughs! Sometimes laughter itself can lighten the burden. Pray this prayer with me.

Precious Father,

I love you, and I pray that you will help me surrender the burdens that I am carrying. Help me to see, know, and understand that I can lay them before you and you will pick them up on my behalf. I thank you for being willing to carry them because, Lord, they are heavy and tiresome. I thank you for placing people around me who love me and want to help me. Jesus already paid the price for my sins and I do not want to cause Him pain by hanging onto sins that have already been forgiven. I want you to take the following burdens and help me to stop picking them back up.

_____

_____

_____

_____

_____

_____

_____

You are an amazing Father, and just as I want to help my children, I know you can and will help me. Thank you for loving me that much.
In Jesus' Precious Name,
Me

Jesus loves children because they solve problems. Jesus loves you!

"I Did It!"
Children Believe They Can Do It!

Matthew 18:2–3

He called a little child and had him stand among them. And He said:
"I tell you the truth, unless you change and become like little children,
you will never enter the kingdom of heaven." (NIV)

He was two years old. He came out of his room one morning beaming with
pride. He had, in fact, dressed himself. He was wearing underwear, backwards,
and it was showing above his shorts, which were turned halfway to the left. His
shirt was on backwards. His right sock was pulled up to midcalf with the heal
bubble on top of his foot, and the left sock was pulled only up to his heal. It was
a sight we have all seen, and we have all had to stifle the laughter within us. I then
squatted down, gave him a big hug, and said, "Great job, honey!" Then, in the
midst of that hug I did as much straightening as I could. There have been many
times since that first "dress himself" experience that Camper has come running
into my room frantic or frustrated because the shirt he was trying to put on did
not have a sleeve that would accommodate his head.

Let us look at the stages of dressing ourselves for just a minute.

1. Mommy dresses us and we are just glad to be warm.
2. We "decide" we can do it ourselves, but sometimes things don't quite fit
   (both legs in one leg hole) or we just are not presentable to be out in
   public.
3. We begin dressing to impress, and sometimes forget our focus (vanity
   and pride get in the way of our day).
4. We realize that we can get away with "bumming" and the only one who
   really has an opinion is mom (apathetic).
5. We have children of our own and often walk into our closet to find
   clothes that are so old that they are coming back into style. Perhaps we
   need some "reviving"!
6. We (hopefully) figure out that our behavior matters more than our
   wardrobe.

Let us look at those stages as they compare to faith:

1. We let our Father tell us and we believe.
2. We decide we can do it ourselves, but we cry and whine to Him when it doesn't work out right, or we get our head stuck in the arm hole.
3. We act "faithful" because it is popular, it is expected, or it is what our friends are doing. We have lost focus.
4. We accept "bumming" or laziness in our faith. We go out into the world in a not-so-presentable manner without concern for how it reflects on our Father.
5. We renew our "faith" for our children's sake or because we are desperately out of touch with today's "Christ-like fashion."
6. We realize that faith and our relationship with our perfect heavenly parent matters more than anything else. Do you remember the first time you realized you were in fact "becoming" your mother? How did you respond? I laughed. Are you actively trying to become more and more like the ultimate parent, Father God?

Become like little children…learn a new task (like dressing yourself), be persistent in the learning process, ask for help when you get your head stuck in the arm hole, share and be proud of what you have learned, give credit to the one who taught us, and practice, practice, practice!

What is the difference between becoming like children and being childish?

_____
_____
_____
_____
_____
_____
_____

Lord Jesus,

I pray that you see in me what you saw in that child. Help me to grow and understand what it means to become like a child. Help me to believe in the gifts you have given me and use them to glorify You.

Love,

Me

Jesus loves children because they believe they can do it! Jesus loves you.

Leap of Faith
Children Trust

Psalm 31:5

Into your hands I commit my spirit; redeem me, O Lord, the God of Truth. (NIV)

Luke 23:46

Jesus called out in a loud voice, "Father into your hands I commit my spirit." When he had said this, he breathed his last. (NIV)

How many of you have encouraged your children to jump to you? Perhaps you cheered them to jump from the bench, from a piece of furniture, or from the side of the pool. The side of the pool is my favorite. You can be less than a foot from them but, for some reason, jumping into the water, where they might go under the water, can be very terrifying.

Kaylyn had just turned six. We were at a friend's house playing in the pool. She wanted to jump from the side but with the condition that my hands were already touching her, that I did not let her go under, and that I promised not to let go. As a parent I said, "Honey, I would never let anything happen to you!" She knew that, but she wanted some reassurance. "Okay, I won't let you go under! Come on…the longer you stand there the scarier it will be."

She jumped…she grabbed on for dear life…she smiled…and then she exclaimed, "I did it!" We all cheered!

As I reflect on the courage it takes to trust someone to catch you I find myself amazed at a child's ability to go ahead and jump. I want to have that courage. I want to be so faithful that God will catch me that I am willing to leap whenever he says, "Go ahead." As Jesus hung on the cross He said, "Into your hands I commit my spirit." That is the ultimate leap of faith. Imagine His Father saying, "Come," and Jesus, having endured torture, humiliation, and rejection, making one final leap for all of us. Imagine God the Father, watching as His Son stood at the edge of death for hours after the beating, the scourging, carrying the weight of the cross, having his hands and feet nailed to that same cross, and hanging there. Jesus waited until God His Father was there, and finally…He Jumped! Thank you, Jesus.

What is the most extreme thing you can see yourself doing for Christ?

_____

_____

_____

_____

_____

_____

_____

What would it take to get you to take that step?

_____

_____

_____

_____

_____

_____

Jesus loves children because they trust. Jesus loves you!

Monkey Bars
Children Practice New Skills

Philippians 4:9

Whatever you have learned or received or heard from me, or seen in me—put it into practice. And the God of peace will be with you. (NIV)

"Mommy, Mommy, I want to do that!"

"Oh, honey, I am not sure you are ready for that."

"Oh, mommy, please, can I try?"

"Honey, I am not sure you can do it."

"I can if you help me!"

"Okay, honey."

She climbs up the ladder to stand on the top bar. Her balance is questionable, and I am holding her waist. She cannot quite reach the first rung. I move around beside her, and I have a choice, lift her—so that she needs me to lift her every time—or tell her to jump—images of her falling race through my mind. I lift her.

As she reaches for the second rung she semi-pleads, "Mommy, hold me up, don't let go!"

"I won't, sweetie," I reassure her.

As she moves her other hand quickly to the second rung I let her dangle a bit, so that she feels her own weight pull against her hands. I wonder if she is really strong enough. She kicks her feet and strains, "Mommy, hold on!!"

"I've got you, you are doing great, keep reaching!"(*instruction*). Suddenly, I am encouraging her to reach for that third rung. I was the voice of skepticism, now I am the voice of *encouragement*. She can succeed…only six and a half rungs to go. She begins to gain a little confidence and makes the left hand, right hand grab to the fourth rung without much trouble. She looks tired. "Are you okay, honey?"

She did not ask for reassurance this time. She *trusts* me. Rung five—no problem. Rung six—takes a couple of swings and hangs for several seconds. *Fast learner!* Rung seven—"Mommy, it's hard"

"You are doing great, you are almost there, hang on and keep moving. I won't let you fall!"

Rung eight, rung nine, "Look, Mommy, I am doing it!" (*confidence*). Rung ten—with a very pointed toe she touches down on the ladder!

"Mommy, Mommy, I did it, did you see me?"

"I am so proud of you! Great job!"

"Can I go again?"

"Okay."

We repeat the process two more times (*practice*), almost exactly as above. On the third repeat I encourage her to jump to the first rung (*leap of faith*). Then, on the fourth repeat, she gains confidence in her own strength and instructs me to, "Just stand there…I can do it, but you won't let me fall will you?"

"No, baby, I won't let you fall!"

She reaches and catches herself on the rung, moves pretty quickly to rung two, then three…a little miss-timing and she dangles. "Mommy, I'm falling!"

"You are okay, I am right here! Go ahead."

"I can't, Mommy, help me! (*Ask for help.*)

As she begins to reach for rung four, *doubt* causes her hand to slip and she falls…I slowed her progression to the ground, and she, through a deep breath, says, "Thanks, mommy. That was scary…I fell but you caught me, huh?"

"I know you fell, but you know what? The more you practice, the easier it will be, and the better you will get at it."

That was almost four years ago! She is a very adept monkey at this point, with rough calloused hands to prove it!

Are there areas in your life where you have been afraid to take a leap of faith? Perhaps a job change or a call to serve God in a way that is way out of your comfort zone? Have you ever wanted to do something and then not done it because you were afraid? Are you afraid to fail? Afraid of what other people might think? Are you afraid because you were not the best?

_____

_____

_____

_____

_____

_____

_____

I love to sing, but it never occurred to me that I might use this gift to glorify God. I decided that I wanted to sing for my son's baptism, and I was terribly nervous. At some point in the preparation for that event, I made a covenant with God that I would only sing in public if it glorified Him, and in turn would He help me not be so nervous? He was faithful, and I continue to keep that covenant.

Camper's baptism was the first time I sang in church. Kaylyn, my four-year-old, sang with me, and she was my angel of calm. God used her to help me not be nervous. At Easter, I sang with no working microphone and just kept going. Several times I have experienced a faith healing of my voice or I've been blessed not to lose it until after a service. One time I sang with my friend Paula, and I managed to tape the music together out of order. (That will definitely test your pianist's ability to ad-lib. I do not recommend it!) That was, thus far, my ultimate humility lesson. Finally, while singing on Good Friday, I was overwhelmed by the words of "Feel the Nails" and completely fell apart. God was my Father in each of those instances and God always blesses what people hear. I am thankful and sing only to glorify Him! It is my sacrifice to Him.

What struggles are you dealing with that you have not trusted your heavenly Father to help you with? More importantly, what skills do you have that, with a little practice, could be used to glorify God?

_____

_____

_____

_____

_____

_____

_____

Let's go back to the monkey bars for a moment.

There you stand, up on the ladder, needing to really stretch for that first rung. You just might have to take a *leap of faith*. He helps you and lifts you to take that first step. As you move tentatively from one rung to the next you feel the weight of your burdens pull against you and He lets you feel that weight.

You check for reassurance that He is really there. He gently whispers *instruction* to you, and that helps you deal with the pressure. "Keep moving, I am right here my child!"

You hear His *encouragement* and keep moving.

As you methodically move forward your *confidence* begins to grow.

Left...right, left...right, left...miss-timing...dangle! Do you call for help? If not, He desperately wants you to speak out to Him. He wants us to *ask for help*. "Help me, I can't do it! I am going to fall!" He reaches up and holds your left hand on the bar so that you can let go of the other bar and bring your hands together. His touch was all you needed to be reassured!

As you get to the end of that journey you reach for the ladder...proud of yourself. Remember to *thank* your loving Father who helped you learn, who kept you safe, and who never left your side.

"Are you ready to try again?" He asks. Are you willing to *practice*?

"Yes, Father, but you will protect me, right?"

"Yes, my child! I am here. I will help you."

Jesus loves children because they practice new skills. Jesus loves you.

No Shame
Children Are *Not* Ashamed

Luke 9:26

If anyone is ashamed of me and my words, the Son of Man will be ashamed of him when he comes in his glory and in the glory of the Father and of the holy angels. (NIV)

Do you have a toddler who just really prefers to be naked? My son is definitely one of those children. One day after his bath he informed me, in his two-and-a-half-year-old voice of authority, that he was going to get his pajamas. I responded, "Great, bring them to the living room. I am going to check with Daddy about dinner." I opened the door to the back yard to go speak with Daddy and right behind me is my cute little boy in nothing but a hat and proud of it. He darts out into the yard and is as pleased as punch with himself that he has managed to escape the house naked.

On a second occasion I had several church friends over one Saturday morning to work on a Bible study and complete a scripture walk. My children were still in their pajamas when I mistakenly asked them to go get dressed. I am thankful that they were eager to comply in front of company but compliance backfired a tad. I accompanied my daughter to her room to get her clothes from her closet while the following scene transpired on the other side of my house. My son proceeded to strip off his clothes and walk through the living room to put them in the laundry room (a good thing). He then sauntered from the laundry room back through the living room toward his bedroom. As I returned to the living room, my guests were chuckling (in the "I really want to heehaw but I will contain myself" kind of chuckle). My son came down the hall to make his third entrance, now needing help to retrieve the clothes from his closet. I laughed and blushed at the same time, scooped him up and left my friends in a fit of laughter.

Following both of these situations I had to realize he was *not* ashamed! This was originally how God intended for our relationship with Him to be. It was after the first sin that two adults covered themselves and were ashamed of their nakedness. Now, I am not saying that we should be like our kids and run around naked to prove that we have nothing to be ashamed of, but we must realize that we should not be ashamed before our heavenly Father. He loves us more than I love my shameless child. He chuckles when our actions are innocent and unafraid. He smiles with pride at how cute we are in our innocence and lack of knowledge.

We are forgiven and we cannot hide anything from our Father, just as our kids usually can't hide things from us. I do not want my children to be ashamed before me. I do not want my children to be ashamed of me. I do not want to shame my children. Guess what? God is the same way. We must be shameless in our faith. We must show it, live it, and honor it. We must proclaim Jesus Christ as the Risen Lord. Silence is perceived as shame, and I will, on a daily basis, try to model after my children who are *not* ashamed!

Jesus loves children because they are *not* ashamed. Jesus loves you!

"What Is It?"
Children Wonder

2 Corinthians 9:15

Thanks be to God for his indescribable gift! (NIV)

Imagine your toddler or young child, and remember a time when he received a gift that he either did not like, did not know what it was, or thought was just weird. How did he react? Did he make a funny face...ugly face...disappointed face? Did he actually ask, "What is it?" Do you recall, as a child, getting a present from grandma and not reacting the way your mother wanted you to, so you were lucky enough to receive a thump on the head?

Grandparents are notorious for giving sentimental and valuable gifts that children just do not understand at the time! How do we as parents expect our children to respond? Is it embarrassing when our children appear ungrateful? Children are full of wonder and amazement when it comes to gifts. Children wonder, "What it is?" out loud. Children wonder, "Why it is special?" Children wonder, "What does it do? What is for?"

How do you think Jesus, when He was a two-year-old toddler, responded when the Magi brought him the following gifts?

"Gold...wwooowww! How pwitty and shiny. I wanna play."

"Frankincense...yucky! Mommy it stinks."

"Myrrh...can I have some?"

I can imagine him being cute with his response because my son at two years old thought three pennies was a lot of money. I love that he appreciates shiny things. I can imagine Jesus looking at the gold, wanting to run to his piggy bank, having no real need for all that money. Jesus would live a life of necessity, and had no real use for excess material items. Children, like Jesus, are able to find wonder in simple things. Remember the empty box at Christmas that your children would play with for hours in shear delight. Our Father in heaven gave us the most incomprehensible gift. He gave His son, on a cross, which would pay all the debts we could ever rack up in sin. Jesus is the most valuable gift ever given. How are we responding to that gift? Are we full of wonder and amazement? Are we grateful? I am certain that I have sinned this week and do not always think twice about the debt that has already been paid on my behalf. Our sin is forgiven. The debts are paid in full. I hope that we are like those children who appreciate the simple gifts, and wonder in amazement at the awesome gifts. It is kind of like the savings bond your grandmother purchased for you when you were born that might mature sometime before you die. It doesn't have value until much later. Jesus' crucifixion is a gift that we cannot fully realize the value of until much later. Jesus' gift will reach full maturity when we die and step into eternity with Him.

Perhaps you accepted the gift of salvation some time in the past. Perhaps you have yet to accept it and ask Jesus into your heart. Either way, today we can renew our "Savings Bond" and cash it in for eternity. Confess with your mouth that you have racked up a debt and you now realize that you can never pay it off. Ask Jesus to come into your heart and to make it new. My precious friend in Christ, your debt is now paid in full!

Jesus loves children because they wonder. Jesus loves you.

ANGEL MOMENTS

Angel moments are those that touch your heart at its core. They bring the bursting with pride, tears ready to fall, and face hurting smiles all in the same moment. I have been blessed to see my children as tiny angels without wings. During a crisis they always seem to know when a hug is needed. They will say, "I love you," at the exact moment when life seems unbearable. They can share the purest of compliments and the most perfect observations. Children are, in those moments, a beautiful miracle sent directly from a Father who loves us beyond words. It is in a child's character to serve. They leave their mark, and they value creation. Children are affectionate, and they see beauty in a sometimes ugly world. A child will accept comfort when they are hurting. They have pure hearts and rest peacefully. Perhaps most importantly…children reach with all the fervor and love of Jesus Christ.

Battle to Serve
Children Serve

Matt 28:18–19

Then Jesus came to them and said, "All authority in heaven and on earth has been given to me. Therefore go and make disciples of all nations, baptizing them in the name of the Father and of the Son and of the Holy Spirit. (NIV)

My precious children often find themselves in a battle to serve their daddy. Daddy will ask one of them to bring a soda from the refrigerator, and, if the other child is anywhere within earshot, the race is on! They both sprint to the kitchen yelling at each other.

"I wanna gidit!"

"No, Camper, Daddy asked me to get it!"

Sometimes it gets a little rough—a push, a shove, a holler, "Mommy!!! Kaylyn won't let me do it!" and I wonder how I even got involved.

We chuckle to ourselves realizing that this strong desire to serve may not last forever, but for now it is quite entertaining. Where does their passion to serve come from? Where does it go when it seems to disappear? Rick will sometimes whisper his request in Camper's ear in order that he might have a slight head start on his big sister. If she figures it out, though, the race begins again! It is really an amazing testament to children. They will knock each other over in order to serve their father, who, by the way, is perfectly capable of getting out of the recliner and getting a drink for himself! Picture God, in heaven, on His throne (perhaps it is an old green recliner), and He gives all authority to Jesus Christ, and in response He runs into a broken world, cold and full of rotten stuff (like the refrigerator) and chooses to offer Himself as the sacrifice for our sins. He makes a simple request while He is here among us…go get me disciples and baptize them! Angela, how about you? How about you? Are we jumping up to say, "No let me!" "I'll do it!" "No He picked me!" "But I wanna go!" "But it's my turn!" Are we even making a remote attempt to help those who are serving Him faithfully?

How can we do a better job serving starting right now?

_____
_____
_____
_____
_____
_____
_____
_____
_____
_____
_____
_____
_____
_____
_____
_____
_____
_____
_____
_____

Jesus loves children because they serve! Jesus loves you!

Cement Handprints
Children Leave Their Mark

<u>Deuteronomy 7:6</u>

For you are a people holy to the Lord your God. The Lord your God has chosen you out of all the peoples on the face of the earth to be his people, his treasured possession. (NIV)

How many of you have either a cement handprint or hand art somewhere in your house that was made by one of your children or grandchildren? Do you remember how old he or she was when it was made? Do you remember the first one you received from your child that he or she made at school? Why is it that we treasure these little trinkets? Take a second or two and write about a special trinket that you treasure from a special child.

_____

_____

_____

_____

_____

_____

Those tiny treasures help us remember how tiny our children once were. They mark growth. They are a little part of them. They are precious because they were made by them and of them. They are priceless and wonderful. We can touch them and feel their tiny hands in ours and we recall the fat little playdough hands and feet. We can reflect on the memories of trying to get that tiny, curled up hand to open up just long enough to mash it into some gooey substance so that we could immortalize that unique little handprint.

Do you think Mary had some tiny handprint of Jesus as a baby boy? Jesus must have been a precious little boy, curious and amazing in knowledge of things beyond His years. Do you suppose He loved to play in Joseph's shop? I can imagine Him getting into things as a typical boy would do and leaving tiny hand prints everywhere! I wonder if Mary, after watching her son be brutalized and crucified, took her precious child from the cross and held Him. Did she reach to hold His lifeless hand, now bearing the wound caused by a nail, and remember those times when he was a child? When we look at our children's hand and foot-prints do we remember that there once was a mother who's "perfect" little boy became a "perfect man" who's "perfect hands and feet" are forever scarred by nails that were placed there for each of our sins?

We were chosen to receive God's perfect gift. He handed us Jesus because each of us is a treasured possession. You are handpicked. Reach out and touch Jesus, and when He reaches to you, remember that there is no handprint more beautiful or perfect than that of the one with a nail scar taken voluntarily for your freedom from sin. If you have never accepted the gift of Jesus then I encourage you to take that step now. It is as simple as saying, "I am a sinner! Forgive me Lord! I accept Jesus as my Savior and King and desire His presence in my heart!" If you will say those words, I would love to be the first to welcome you to the family! Welcome!

Jesus loves children because they leave their mark. Jesus loves you.

"Holy Poly"
Children Value Creation

<u>Matthew 25:45</u>

He will reply, "I tell you the truth, what ever you did not do for one of the least of these, you did not do for me." (NIV)

It was early one morning in May and my two-and-a-half-year-old son and I were headed out the door. As I got to the car I turned around to see my son stop, put his hands on his knees, and squat down. He was intently talking to a roly poly. He first said, "Coooolll!" His second comment was more of an instruction to me, "Look, Mommy, a holy poly!"

I should have known right then that there was a lesson in this somewhere. I chuckled and then he squinted his tiny eyes and yelled, "Hey, don't go thaaauu-ure!" He was instructing the misguided little critter to stay clear of his shoe.

Now these critters are everywhere at certain times of the year, and my precious son is fascinated with them. He is very sweet and will move them to safety quite frequently. I remember speaking to parents who chuckled as they recalled their own little hero saving thirty "holy polys" from this harsh world by placing them in his pockets. This morning, though, my view was a little different. The verse in Matthew 25:45 invaded my thoughts.

I could imagine Jesus teaching his disciples about love and using a child, who grasped the concept of love far better than most adults. Children will protect, value, and cherish the least of all creatures on this planet (roly polys, rocks, lady-bugs, flowers, etc.). There are many people who do not "deserve" grace or mercy because they are mean or infectious or because they just plain suck the life out of all those around them. There are people who have taken advantage of our kind-ness, our charity, our generosity, and our time. There are those who have gossiped and betrayed us, those who have hurt the people trying to help them, and those who are just angry, bitter, and resentful and don't want help. (Sound familiar???) Oh wait—I just described myself and my relationship with Jesus. I deserve nothing from Him, but He gave everything anyway.

Jesus wants each of us to never stop being childlike. He tells us this several times.

I don't know about you, but until that moment watching my son, roly polys (or as he says, holy polys) have always fallen into the category of "least," "least deserving," or "least significant," and yet my son gently and adoringly coaxed at least one little critter to move in a path that was less dangerous.

Imagine God, our Father, squatting down, gently calling to the least deserving of people (Saul comes to mind) and saying "Cooolll! Look at him! No, no don't go thaaauuure! Go this way. Let me take care of you, guide you, and use you as you are, in your weakness and insignificance, to bless the lives of those around you." Be blessed the next time you see a "holy poly." Better yet, when you are confronted with that person who in your heart does not deserve your time, your help, your compassion, or your patience…think to yourself, this person is my "holy poly" and choose

1. To be like a child.
2. To love like Christ.
3. To respond with love because Christ said so.

Think for a moment about the people who probably fall into this category in your life. I want you to pray for them each day this week and pray that your attitude toward those people or that person will change. Write a possible prayer for them.

_____
_____
_____
_____
_____
_____
_____

Jesus loves children because they value creation. Jesus loves you!

"I Have a Secret"
Children Are Affectionate

Deuteronomy 10:15

Yet the Lord set his affection on your forefathers and loved them, and he chose you, their descendants, above all the nations, as it is today. (NIV)

Kaylyn was big into secrets and whispering in my ear. She would usually run up to me saying, "I have a secret, Mommy," pull me by the hand until I got down on her level, use both hands to cover my ear, and then say, "I love you"—and usually she would say it loud enough for anyone within five feet to hear. She would chuckle with pride and then lean toward me anxiously waiting for me to whisper to her "Kaylyn, I love you!" What made this even more adorable was that she would return within a couple of minutes to repeat the process. I don't know about you, but those are precious memories for me. Kaylyn is now six and she still often and visibly shows affection. There is something in a child's sincerity that just makes life worth living! I do not know how long she will continue to want to hold my hand, tell me in front of her friends that she loves me, give me hugs and kisses for no reason, or be so sweet as to say without thinking, "Mommy, you are so pretty!," but I know that in those moments I love everything about my life.

I find myself wondering if my Father in heaven longs to recapture our early days of faith when we would proudly proclaim our love for Him. Does He miss the times when we would often and visibly show our affection and sincerely demonstrate our love for Him? Does He even remember when we longed to be hugged by Him? Think for a moment about that tiny precious secret…"I love you!" Is it a secret that we share only with Him, or do we "whisper" so that everyone within five feet can hear us?

In a journal that I put together I was encouraging my friends to write a letter to God. I asked them to write to Him as if they were adoring children. You can do this, too. Tell Him what you love about Him and about what He has given you. Tell Him about all the beautiful creations you see in your surroundings and any other details you have on your heart.

Dear "Dad,"

_____

_____
_____
_____
_____
_____
_____
_____
_____
_____
_____
_____
_____
_____
_____
_____
_____
_____
_____
_____
_____
_____
_____
_____
_____
_____
_____
_____
_____
_____
_____
_____
_____
_____
_____
_____
_____

With all my heart,
Me

Jesus loves children because they are affectionate. Jesus loves you.

"Look! It's Bwuutiful!"
Children See Beauty!

<u>Ecclesiastes 3:11</u>

He has made everything beautiful in its time. He has also set eternity in the hearts of men; yet they cannot fathom what God has done from beginning to end. (NIV)

I have the glorious privilege of seeing the world through the eyes of my children, and sometimes what they see is astounding. During volleyball season, I was working really long hours. One morning, before daylight, as I was taking my son to his daycare, he squealed from the backseat, "Look mommy, fiuquackas!"

I glanced at him and he was looking up at the stars in the sky! I smiled and cried in the same moment because I was overwhelmed by how sad it was that I was leaving my son before the sun came up but how awesome it was for God to have given me that glimpse of heaven in my backseat! After an infinite pause I replied, "Yep, those are God's fireworks, aren't they beautiful?"

He did not respond. He simply looked into that darkness as if God put them there just for us. He did!

On another occasion, I was again taking Camper to daycare. We were late, and I was irritated. We turned to cross over the railroad tracks and from the mouth of my son came these words, "Mommy, look at the bwuutiful colors, sooo pwiddy!"

I again had to look at him to see what could have inspired such sweet words. He was describing the most spectacular sunrise I have ever seen. I had not even noticed! Reduced to sucking back the tears through a smile, I thought to myself "Okay, God, I get it...thank you." I then turned to my son to tell him, "I love you," and he responded in kind. I decided right then (and it was a decision) that it would be a good day, no matter what!

Jesus must take great pleasure in these moments when my children become my teacher. I thank you, Lord, for my children. I see Jesus in them every day. Help me to teach them, love them, and guide them in their walk with You. These two experiences were the inspiration for the song *Thank You for the Son-Rise*, that maybe someday I will have the opportunity to share with you, but until that time I have included the lyrics here. As you read them, I want you to see and to know that Jesus is the Son, the beginning, and the end. Jesus is the giver of life and the bright and shining star that shines on us, in us, and through us.

What if you suddenly could not see? Would you have taken in enough of God's beautiful creation to last until you meet your Father in heaven? What if your child was robbed of his or her sight or hearing? Would you be able to duplicate their beautiful observations of all of God's wonders for them?

Take a minute and describe the most beautiful image you have in your memory bank. Try to describe what makes it so wonderful. Think of the perfect way a child might describe that scene.

_____

_____

_____

_____

_____

_____

_____

Jesus loves children because they see beauty! Jesus loves you.

Thank You for the Son-Rise

Lyrics by: Angela Kirkpatrick
Music by: Chad Johnson

Have you ever watched a sunset as it gently says goodnight?
The world turns it's back on it. It sets without a fight.
Have you ever seen a sunrise at the start of each new day?
It rises in its glory, sometimes we forget to say…

Thank you for the light you shine upon this world so dim.
Thank you that you're always there, the beginning and the end.
Thank you for the life you give to all things both near and far.
Thank you for your beauty. You're the bright and shining star.

Like the beauty of the sunset one night so long ago.
They wrapped and set the Son inside a tomb made out of stone.
As they wept and cried with sadness that this Son-set might last,
The Son would rise in glory after three short days had passed.
One day they watched the Son set as He gently said "goodnight."
The world turned its back on Him. He "set" without a fight.
So when you see the Son-rise at the start of each new day.
He is risen in His Glory, so don't forget to say…

Thank you for the light you shine upon this world so dim.
Thank you that you're always there, the beginning and the end.
Thank you for the life you give to all things both near and far.
Thank you for your beauty. You're the bright and shining star.

And one day I'll get to heaven and I'll see the risen Son.
I'll wake to spend eternity in the glory of the One.
And as He draws me close to Him to live forever more.
I hope I think to thank Him for the Son will set no more.
And one day we'll get to heaven and we'll see the risen Son.
We'll wake to spend eternity in the glory of the One.
And as He draws us close to Him to live forever more.
I hope we think to thank Him for the Son will set no more.

I hope I think to thank Him for the Son will set no more.

"Mommy, Kiss It"
Children Accept Comfort

Isaiah 66:13

As a mother comforts her child, so will I comfort you. (NIV)

He ran smack into the coffee table. He was running and should not have been. It knocked him down, and he looked for my reaction. Because I broke a cardinal rule and gasped, he proceeded to work himself into a blood-curdling scream. Now, because I reacted, I had to fix it. So I walked over to him, sat down next to him, and asked if it needed a "mommy kiss." They are, of course, magical in the eyes of a child. I kissed it and he "snuffled-up." I hugged him and it was all better.

Another time he came in from the backyard after falling down on the side-walk. He was holding his knee, crying uncontrollably, and asking for a Band-Aid. There was no actual evidence of a fall on either leg (it must be nice to be two feet tall), and I weighed my options. If I said, "You don't need a Band-Aid," the fit would continue. If I gave it to him with no "blood" it would cost a mini-fortune to put Band-Aids on every boo-boo. I asked if a kiss would work, and he replied, "No, I wanna Scooby-Doo Band-Aid." Well, I did give it to him (Choose your battles!) and I was thankful that he really was not hurt.

Have any of your children ever had a boo-boo that you just could not fix? That is a very helpless feeling. I do not have the answer to that, other than preparing my children in a very real way to rely on Jesus through the pain. I would like to share with you two mini-stories of two very special children who have eternally touched my heart. Katy was a student of mine at Copperas Cove. Katy has Cerebral Palsy, and her tiny, frail, and deteriorating body carries her with great effort. I asked my students to write a speech. The topic was "An Important Lesson I Have Learned," and this is what she wrote, exactly as she wrote it.

"Are you the person that wishes you were a different person, or are you the person that realized you are special just the way you are? I remember a couple of months ago that I hated having a disability and wished I could be like everybody else. Then, I realized after I volunteered a couple of times that I have a purpose in life, and even though I have a disability, I can have a huge impact on peoples lives. I didn't think that people who are not disabled can have bigger problems than I do. The next time you think you are not special or wish you were someone else, just remember God made you for a reason."

Katy knows the heart of Jesus, and even though life is tough for her, she "gets it"!

Are we taking our children to the Word of God to get a Band-Aid, medicine, or therapy they need to feel better? Are we role-modeling a trust in our Father (as they trust us) to make both the physical and emotional boo-boos better? Reflect for a moment on a time when you needed to feel God's loving strength for a boo-boo that was at the time unbearable.

_____

_____

_____

_____

_____

_____

_____

The second story I want to share is about Josiah. He is, without a doubt, my hero. This precious boy, at nine, was losing his battle with brain cancer. His daddy faithfully kept people posted via e-mail, and in their e-mails they brought countless people back to the cross of Jesus as they allowed us to suffer with them through this tragedy. One particular e-mail touched my heart forever, and I got permission to share a part of it with you.

From Bull (daddy)
"Josiah has been like a snow man that is melting away before our eyes. Kelly has been hurting as she is near him daily. (A few days ago) I was called directly from work to the hospital, no time to change out of my uniform. The trip up was not dry…many tears and prayers. When I arrived, Josiah appeared in a fog. I personally felt he had but a few hours left to live. I still stand firm on the moving of the LORD most high!…Josiah has lost nearly 90–95% use of his right arm and leg. He is at home now and not stuck in the hospital. It is hard as he has moments where he tries to talk but the words are on delay or lost. Then he has moments of conversation. He has lost interest in trying to read, write, or even color as his mind tries one thing and his right arm does not operate at all any more in regard to motor skills. But Josiah can still pray 'Dear heavenly Father, please do not let those reading this get hurt and help them make things right. In Jesus name…Amen (hold your eyes closed for five seconds. Josiah says this helps the prayer)'…He is going back to sleep now."…

For several months I cried every time I read those words. Josiah prayed for me in that moment. Josiah prayed for you in that moment. Josiah is now celebrating and singing praise to his Lord almighty as he stands without pain at the throne of God. Jesus loves these two precious angels. Jesus commands that we be like them. They know that the only source of comfort in this sometimes cruel world is in the safe strong arms of their Father in heaven. When a child demonstrates faith, it creates in me an overwhelming feeling of humility. Each of us is worthy of our Father's love. We simply have to be like that child who will "accept" the comfort He is willing to give.

What areas do we need to surrender to our loving Father that only he has the magic Band-Aid or that loving kiss to make it better?

_____

_____

_____

_____

_____

_____

_____

Lord Jesus,

Help me learn from these, Your precious children. Help me run to you for comfort and accept it when it is offered. I know you do not cause me pain but that pain happens on this earth. I thank you for those big broad shoulders to cry on when it hurts and I am not sure I can take anymore. Thank you for placing people in my life that love me enough to help me through the hurt, and help me be aware of those around me who need to see your loving eyes through me.

In Your Name,

Me

Jesus loves children because they accept comfort. Jesus loves you.

Pure in Heart
Children Have Pure Hearts

<u>Matthew 5:8</u>

Blessed are the pure in heart, for they will see God! (NIV)

This has to be one of the greatest truths in the Bible, and this is how I know. On two separate occasions my six-and-a-half-year-old daughter proved it beyond a shadow of a doubt.

One Sunday in September 2004, Kaylyn, from the back seat, said, "Mommy, we're all a part of God's body somehow—right?"

Stunned by her question, I responded, "Yes you are right, honey!"

"Do you know what part you are?" she inquired.

"Well, I guess I am not sure," I replied, realizing that was an uninspiring answer.

I glanced back at my pensive daughter, and she responded, "Well, I hope I'm His heart!"

Through proud tears I could barely muster, "Oh, honey, me too!"

In October of 2004, we were again in the car but on our way to school. Kaylyn began with a question. "Mommy, is the Easter Bunny real?" Of course she asked this with her three-year-old brother sitting next to her.

So I cautiously said, "Well, what do you think?"

She replied, "I think Mimi and Gramma hide the eggs (pause), and I've never seen it."

"Well, you have never seen Santa." I said.

Kaylyn quickly responded, "Yeah, but who else would stay up all night delivering toys?"

I smiled! Enter God into my thoughts so that I might, in all my wisdom, make this a teachable moment. You know, the doubting-Thomas lesson. So I began, thinking I was going to set her up, and I said, "Well, you've never seen Jesus."

She responded, "Yes I have!!" in a semi shout.

Uh-oh, I think. "Oh, really?" I said, truly interested in what she was going to say.

"Yes, I see Him in my heart!"

I was silent and humbled.

Thank You!

Holy Father,

I love that You are perfect and pure and a wonderful example to all of your children. I pray, Lord, that in those moments when my children humble me that I, too, can experience a love so deep that I can know without a doubt that you are in my heart. I pray that You will help me let down any barriers that I have created that might be separating me from You.

In Jesus' Precious Name,

Me

Jesus loves children because they are pure in heart. Jesus loves you!

As I reflect on the perfect nature of a child's understanding of our heart, I want to include a segment of a lesson that I did in my *Steps to Faith* program as a way to understand more of our body and how that correlates to a productive church—the Body of Christ.

Anatomy 101 "Bible Style"

By Angela Kirkpatrick for my friends in *Steps to Faith*

Nervous System—"Control Center"
God is in control, and this is both a voluntary and involuntary relationship.
Respiratory System—"Air Exchange"
Worship Jesus! He is the air we breathe. When He took His last, we took our first!
Immune System—"Protection"
God's angels and the Holy Spirit protect us.
Skeletal System—"Framework"
Our Church Building…Is it solid and strong enough to support the body?
Muscular System—"Voluntary Movement"
Members of our church must choose to *move*!
Integument System—"Covering"
Prayer covers a multitude of sins and binds us together.
Digestive System—"Nourishment"
Bible Study and time with God is all we really need.
Urinary System—"Filter Waste"
Spiritual "waste" often comes from our mouths. Self Control is the filter. *Use it*!
Cardiovascular System—"Transport Air/Nutrients"
Missionaries/Evangelists who transport Jesus & the Word of God
To the rest of the body and to the *world*!
Endocrine/Lymphatic System—"Regulators"
Church Leadership, tithes, and committees that are
necessary to keep the church moving.
Reproductive System—"Passing our traits to the next Generation"
What Christ-like traits have we passed on to our children?

LJPPKGFGSc—Of course, I had to include it!

Sleep Like a Baby
Children Rest Peacefully

Matthew 11:28

Come to me, all you who are weary and burdened, and I will give you rest. (NIV)

Camper must have been about eighteen months old when I came into the living room from doing the dishes and found him crashed out on the floor, legs and arms tucked under him, diaper bottom sticking straight up in the air. The TV was blaring, Kaylyn was talking to me, and there he slept. When I look into the face of a sleeping child, I see that peace beyond all understanding, and I see the face of God. When my children sleep, you can vacuum outside their rooms, set the house alarm off, mow outside their window, and leave the phone on their bed by accident and have it ring and not wake them. Children always know when enough is enough. Jesus, I am sure, desires that we stop, rest, and listen. I have had fitful nights of thoughts. I have had nights when I worry all night about something that I have absolutely no control over. I have gone to bed upset and awakened tired and more upset because I chose to hang on to those emotions throughout the night. When children have night terrors or bad dreams, mommy and daddy can sometimes make it better simply by walking into the room. Other times they come to our room to be comforted by the opportunity to hop into bed with us. My children then proceed to sleep sideways between us, feet and arms draped on our heads, perfectly content and immediately asleep.

This verse represents what children do. Children come to us when they are tired or stressed, and we hope to provide them the comfort they need. Sleep can be a time of renewal, and I am quite sure that our Father in heaven looks at us while we peacefully sleep and gently strokes our face. He loves us beyond words, beyond tears, and beyond eternity. Rest and feel Him with you. The best sleep you will ever get is when you honestly and audibly turn over the stresses of the day to your Father. Let Him rock them away so that sleep will come and peace will be with us—even if we, in our stubbornness, choose to pick those stresses back up again the next morning.

It is time to do a little personal confessing. Give some examples of issues that you have lost sleep over. What are some things that have caused you frustration for which you have awakened at night and in the morning could still feel the emotional, stress-induced exhaustion?

_____

_____

_____

_____

_____

_____

_____

Loving Father,
Help each of us to seek rest and peace in Your strong arms of love. In them we can sleep as a child sleeps.

Jesus loves children because they rest peacefully. Jesus loves you.

"Up"
Children Reach

1 Peter 5:6–7

Humble yourselves, therefore under God's mighty hand, that he may lift you up in due time. Cast all your anxiety on him because he cares for you. (NIV)

Romans 9:17

I raised you up for this very purpose, that I might display my power in you and that my name might be proclaimed in all the earth. (NIV)

Children are precious. There are so many times that I find they instinctively know so much more than I do. Think for a minute about your children/grandchildren. Recall what they were like as infants and toddlers. Can you even begin to imagine how many times you physically picked them up? Care to guess? How about how many times in one day? Ten, twenty-five, fifty?

Let's think for a minute about that "pick-me-up" posture.

Arms fully extended...shoulders shrugged to their ears...fingers wiggling wildly...face full of emotion and anticipation...and completely faithful that we will oblige their request! Right? They do all this with very little verbal ability. They may grunt. They might say, "Up," and sometimes we get excited when we get the full sentence, "Up please!" (Remember *Manners 101?*) Let's think for a minute about why we might have picked up that sweet little angel.

1. "*Up*"—because I hurt myself and I need comfort.
2. "*Up*"—because I am just too tired to go on.
3. "*Up*"—because I am scared of the monster in my room.
4. "*Up*"—because he snatched it and it's mine.
5. "*Up*"—because I don't want to share you anymore.
6. "*Up*"—because I want to cry on your shoulder because life isn't fair.
7. "*Up*"—because I am sad and upset.
8. "*Up*"—because I am so glad to see you.
9. "*Up*"—because I want to see things from way up there.
10. "*Up*"—because I can't reach it myself.

11. "*Up*"—because I just need some reassurance of your love.
12. "*Up*"—because I want to touch your face (my favorite).
13. "*Up*"—because I want to show you how much I love you.
14. "*Up*"—because I want you to know you are the best.
15. "*Up*"—because *You reached for me first!*

Did I miss any that you can think of? The hands are the same. The word is the same. We never grow tired of granting this request (well, maybe) but we certainly never want them to quit asking, even when we physically cannot lift them anymore, right? So why would we think our Father in heaven is any different?

Then take comfort in knowing that He wants to lift us up. Close your eyes. Bow your head for a moment, and then lift your head toward heaven and feel the warmth and the light. As we reflect together on when we might need to lift our hands to our Father, read each one and be encouraged that He, too, wants to lift us up in every circumstance.

1. "*Up*"—because I hurt myself, and I need comfort.
2. "*Up*"—because I am just too tired to go on.
3. "*Up*"—because I am scared of the monster in my room.
4. "*Up*"—because he snatched it and it's mine.
5. "*Up*"—because I don't want to share you anymore.
6. "*Up*"—because I want to cry on your shoulder because life isn't fair.
7. "*Up*"—because I am sad and upset.
8. "*Up*"—because I am so glad to see you.
9. "*Up*"—because I want to see things from way up there.
10. "*Up*"—because I can't reach it myself.
11. "*Up*"—because I just need some reassurance of your love.
12. "*Up*"—because I want to touch your face (my favorite).
13. "*Up*"—because I want to show you how much I love you.
14. "*Up*"—because I want you to know you are the best.
15. "*Up*"—because *You reached for me first!*

God wants us to reach up to Him. Sometimes we throw our hands up in frustration or surrender. Sometimes we don't lift our hands to Him in worship because of what those around us might think, or because, like a teenager, it is not cool to show that kind of affection. It is an act of worship and humility to raise your hands to your almighty Father. Keep your eyes closed…and raise your hands up if He is worthy of your prayers, your praise, and your thanksgiving. Hands up…because right at this moment you want Him to reach down and touch you, to comfort you, and to remain in you. Hands up…because I want you to know you are worthy of His love. Hands up…because Jesus raised His in surrender to the Roman guards and voluntarily raised them to be nailed to a cross on our behalf. Hands up…my dear brothers and sisters, because your Father in heaven is right at this moment *reaching for you first!*

If I could sing for you in this moment, I would sing "He Raised Me Up" and then share with you the verse from Romans 9:17.

Jesus loves children because they reach "*Up*"! Jesus loves you.

I love and thank my children for teaching me to do the same.

MOMENTS MADE FOR FUN AND GAMES

These are the moments in life when child rearing is just plain fun. I love to play with my children. I firmly believe it is good for the soul, and my spirit celebrates the memories that accompany those times together. Music also has a huge role in my house. I sing all of the time, and I seem to have passed that to my children. We spend hours singing, making up silly songs like *Monkey Bar Adventure*, and learning to allow our hearts to rejoice with the words we use to praise God. In these moments of fun and games, God sometimes reaches into my brain to pull out a scriptural truth by which I can learn some important lesson. Children know who's in control, and they are willing to follow. Children are competitive and learn early how to pick a good team. Children love to dress up, and even the heavenly angels smile when children make joyful noise. Children go when the light is green, and they love stories. As you read, enjoy and be lifted up by a God who desires to have that same playful, wonderful relationship with you.

Daddy's Chair—Children Know Who's in Control
Follow the Leader—Children Follow
Last Picked—Children Pick to Win
Let's Play Dress-Up—Children Dress Up
"Mary Had a Little Lamb"—Children Make a Joyful Noise!
"Red Light, Green Light"—Children *Go*!
Wonderful Tales—Children Love Stories

Daddy's Chair
Children Know Who's in Control

2 Chronicles 20:6

O Lord, God of our fathers, are you not the God who is in heaven? You rule over all the kingdoms of the nations. Power and might are in your hand, and no one can withstand you. (NIV)

How many of your homes have a "daddy chair"? My children love to be in Daddy's chair. It is an oversized, overstuffed green recliner that has been Rick's chair for at least twelve years now. It is comfortable and perfectly suited to him. When he comes in, whoever is sitting in it usually gets out letting him sit down. My kid's think it's cute, once in a while, to hop into it before him just to see what kind of reaction they can provoke. Usually he will playfully sit on them until they eventually relent. Sometimes he raises an eyebrow and they will quickly hop out, and on really bad days, he will command them to get out.

I, twice in one month, heard analogies to sitting in God's chair. One presenter simply put a sign on a plain old chair that said "God's chair" and invited anyone who wanted to come sit in it to come on up. No one moved.

Rubye Kelly presented it from the following perspective. When I am sitting in God's chair I have to see what He sees. I am deciding what is best instead of asking for guidance and I get mad when He is not helping me. Finally, God taps me on the shoulder and says, "I am right here and you are sitting in *my* chair!"

She responds, "I was just keeping it warm for you."

God replies, "I don't need your help keeping it warm."

We struggle daily wanting to take our Father's place in His chair. My husband has control of the TV from his chair, but God has a grasp on every situation in this world from His chair. We call it the *THRONE OF GLORY!* My kids think that *he who sits in the recliner of glory has the remote control!* For us, we need to remember that *He who sits on the throne of glory has absolute control!*

The movie *Bruce Almighty* was a fantastic analogy for what can happen when we are in control, and it was not good. Bruce ultimately figured out that it was not about him, and in the end he did realize that God was in control and much better suited for the task. We think that we want control, and yet blessings seem to come raining down in those times when we surrender the control to God.

Where in your life have you been fighting with God for control?

_____
_____
_____
_____
_____
_____
_____
_____
_____
_____
_____
_____
_____
_____
_____
_____
_____
_____
_____
_____
_____
_____

Jesus loves children because they know who is in control. Jesus loves you!

Follow the Leader
Children Follow

Matthew 16:24

Then Jesus said to his disciples, "If anyone would come after me, he must deny himself and take up his cross and follow me." (NIV)

Do you remember the childhood game of Follow-the-Leader?

I remember fighting over who would get to be the leader, but we would play for what seemed like hours. My kids love to play, and we laugh the most when the leader does things that we either just can't do, or we all look silly doing it. In the name of a game we would do crazy things like hop, jump, squat, crawl around, run, etc. Jesus explains the cost of following Him. We have to put all of our pride, earthly desires, and belongings aside, take up our cross (a feat that only Jesus is capable of doing), and follow Him. He has left this earth, and leaves us to be the leaders for His kingdom, and, in this job description, sometimes we really have to step out of our comfort zone and obey only Him. We have accepted that people are going to laugh at us. They will judge us. They will persecute us, and they will reject us. As children we just didn't care, and following the leader meant we could blame our craziness on the leader. There is a time and a place to lead in faith, and Jesus our leader wants us to blame Him for our faithful actions and glorify Him with all of our actions.

Think of the people in your church or community who are strong leaders. What is it about those people that make them good leaders?

_____

_____

_____

_____

_____

_____

_____

What are some skills, talents, or gifts that you have that you could be using to expand God's kingdom? It is not humility to put yourself down, so take a moment and be proud of and thankful for the gifts God has given you

_____
_____
_____
_____
_____
_____
_____

Dear Jesus,

Help me each day deny myself. Help me know what that means, to put my desires and pride aside so that I may serve and glorify You. Help me follow Your example of love and mercy with all those I meet. Help me reach out to those whose cross is heavy and lead them back to You. I trust that You will show me when I am to follow and when I am to lead. Give me the courage and faith to willingly obey when You call me to action.

In Jesus' Name,

Me

Jesus loves children because they follow! Jesus loves you.

Last Picked
Children Pick to Win

1 John 2:1

My dear children, I write this to you so that you will not sin. But if anybody does sin, we have one who speaks to the Father in our defense—Jesus Christ, the Righteous One. (NIV)

"I can't wait; today we are playing kickball at recess. I love kickball! I hope Kevin picks me, he is really good!"

The teacher tells us it is time to go. "Yes" I cheer to myself. I have been looking forward to it all week. Out on the playground, Kevin and Shelley are captains. I don't really know why, but no one ever says anything, so they are always captains. We are circled up, ready to get picked!

Shelley picks first, and she picks Ron. He struts over to her.—First picked is a real honor!

Kevin picks Gayle.—She is the fastest!

Shelley picks Kelley.—Of course, they are best friends.

Kevin picks Don.—He is the best pitcher.

Shelley picks Stephanie.—She is great kicker.

Kevin picks Rick.—Now wait a minute, he is so slow...this is embarrassing!

Shelley picks Jenny.—What? I thought she was my friend!

Kevin picks Raegan.—Great, he thinks I'm not good enough!

Shelley picks Kaylyn.—This stinks, please don't let me be picked last!

Kevin picks Camper.—Oh please, down to two; please pick me, please, please...

Shelley picks Sydnie.—I hate this, I'm never playing this stupid game again.

He did not even say my name. He was stuck with me! I hope someday they know how this feels. I wanted to cry!

Where are you in this scenario? Were you the first picked? Were you always the captain? How did you decide who to pick? Did you pick to win...you know the best kicker, fastest runner, most competitive, best defender? Did you pick your friends first, regardless of their ability? Were you the last picked? Did you avoid the game altogether because it hurt less?

As adults we have to help our children learn to pick their life team. We pray that we will be on that team, but who they pick, and who they pick first, will tell a lot about their priorities. Take a minute and write a prayer over your children and the team that they choose to help them through their life.

_____
_____
_____
_____
_____
_____
_____

We are going to fast-forward a couple of years and find out what happens next.

My teacher this year always picks the captains for kickball. I like it that way because everyone gets a turn. Today it is my turn and I am picking against the big bully that everyone calls Big Red!

I went first, "Rick"
Big red picked Sherry
Kaylyn
BR…JW
Camper
BR…William
Gayle
BR…Suzie
Stephanie
BR…Tracey
Etta
BR…Glen

I am surveying the choices so far and realize that Big Red has all the power, size, strength, speed, athleticism, and ability. I look at who is left and realize I have made a terrible mistake. When I look up, there stands the unpopular, quietest kid in the class. There stood JESUS…sad, heartbroken, and humiliated! He didn't want to be picked last and yet there He stood, waiting in agony for one of us to choose Him. Big Red yells out, "I don't want Him!" I begin to cry. I am so sorry; I know how it feels to be picked last. It feels like someone is driving nails right into your heart!

I shouted, "We want Jesus, He is awesome!" The difference is that Jesus immediately forgave me for waiting so long, and I realize that I will never make that mistake again! Jesus is all I need on my team. He can do it all! He is my friend. He plays great defense. He hits home runs every time! He doesn't make mistakes. He cheers the loudest of anyone I know! He is always a great sport and His team will win! Next time I think maybe He should be the captain…what do you think?

Choose your team wisely! List for yourself who should be on your team and describe any differences between the "should" list and the "actual" current list.

_____

_____

_____

_____

_____

_____

_____

Jesus loves children because they pick to win. Jesus loves you.

Let's Play Dress-Up
Children Dress Up

Ephesians 6:10–18 The Armor of God

Finally, be strong in the Lord and in his mighty power. Put on the full armor of God so that you can take your stand against the devil's schemes…Therefore put on the full armor of God, so that when the day of evil comes, you may be able to stand your ground, and after you have done everything, to stand. Stand firm then, with the belt of truth buckled around your waist, with the breastplate of righteousness in place, and with your feet fitted with the readiness that comes from the gospel of peace. In addition to all this, take up the shield of faith, with which you can extinguish all the flaming arrows of the evil one. Take the helmet of salvation and the sword of the Spirit, which is the word of God. And pray in the Spirit on all occasions with all kinds of prayers and requests. With this in mind, be alert and always keep on praying for all the saints. (NIV)

It was Kaylyn's fourth birthday and she had three little friends over to stay the night. At one point late in the evening I heard the typical giggling that I had been hearing, when all of sudden all four girls came out of Kaylyn's room decked out from head to toe. Each girl had donned a frilly hat or tiara, make-up that was just hilariously applied, sequin-adorned flapper skirts, and pink shoes of some type; jammies were protruding from underneath their elaborate costumes, and each girl wore a boa. They were a sight, and they were proud to have completed their own ensembles. They paraded around for me in my own private preschool fashion show, and then we took pictures of them in all their glory. It was an image that I will remember forever! Kaylyn is all girl. It can never be too pink, too frilly, too feathery, or too shiny. Make-up, dress-up, and hairstyles are still a part of every sleep over. I cannot fathom where she got this desire other than from God, and I have had great fun watching her and her friends come up with some fabulous costumes every time.

In Ephesians we learn of the armor of God, and "dressing up" takes on a whole new meaning. Little girls dress up for fun, to be beautiful, and to pretend. In God's dress-up trunk He teaches us to be brave warriors in the face of battle against the evil one. Truth, righteousness, readiness, faith, salvation, and the Spirit…who of us could possibly fail with each of those characteristics as our attire for the day? Oh, but we in our "maturity" think dressing up is silly and for kids. That could not be further from the truth. I would love nothing more than to have each piece of armor in my house so that when we are under attack we could literally put it on, reflect on the Christ-like characteristic it represents, and go forth into battle without fear. Children are truthful, righteous, ready, and faithful. They need us to show them the way to salvation through Christ and to show them that in Christ we have the Great Counselor to help us.

Can you identify which piece of armor you are in need of the most right now? I pray God's armor over you. I pray that you feel His love and know His desire to protect you.

_____

_____

_____

_____

_____

_____

_____

Jesus loves children because they love to dress up. Jesus loves you.

"Mary Had a Little Lamb"
Children Make a Joyful Noise!

Matthew 21:16

"Do you hear what these children are saying?" they asked Him. "Yes," replied Jesus, "have you never read 'From the lips of children and infants you have ordained praise'?" (NIV)

I love to hear my children sing and one day my toothless five-year-old daughter and my two-and-a-half-year-old son were having what seemed to be a musical duel. She was singing *Mary Had a Little Lamb* and Camper piped in with *Jesus Loves Me*. I would like to do a little experiment.

I want you to sing *Mary Had a Little Lamb* to the tune of *Jesus Loves Me*, and then reverse it. Then I want you to alternate lines of each song. Oh, and I want you to sing as if Jesus was sitting next to you and has personally asked you to sing for Him. On three, ready one, two, three.

Was it hard to concentrate? Did you mess up or stop singing? Did you find yourself meandering between the correct tune and lyrics? It's funny, we know the song but we can't always deliver it when we are distracted, can we? That is the state I found myself in when they were singing, but they did not seem to have any trouble…they would simply sing louder!

As I chuckled at them and their sweetness I realized two things. First, children are fully capable of sticking to a point. Second, I learned that we must really work to keep the songs fresh in our head, and that *Mary Had a Little Lamb* could use a little tweaking…

Mary had a little lamb, little lamb, little lamb…
Mary had a little lamb…whose fleece was white as snow.
And every time that lamb did speak, lamb did speak, lamb did speak…
Every time that lamb did speak…More people came to know.
He died upon the cross one day, cross one day, cross one day…
He died upon the cross one day…To save us from our sin.
And then He rose up from the grave, from the grave, from the grave
And then He rose up from the grave…Now I am born again!

Jesus loves children because they make joyful noise. Jesus loves you.

"Red Light, Green Light"
Children *Go*!

Isaiah 30:21

Whether you turn to the right or to the left, you ears will hear a voice behind you saying, "This is the way; walk in it." (NIV)

Remember playing the childhood game Red Light-Green Light? I remember playing and my children love to play. I also learned about this scripture from a scene that transpired when Kaylyn was two-and-a-half years old. She had no fear of anything, and if not restrained, she would run off and be gone in an instant. Any of you have children like that? Gray hair at twenty-eight years old, yeah, that was me with Kaylyn. One day we were in a crowded mall and she darted out in front of me. I did not want to yell her name because, even though she had no fear, I had an abundance of fear. So I, in my infinite weirdness, hollered *"red light!"*

She, in her not quite three-year-old coordination, took two more steps and then froze in a leaning-forward-to-start-the-race position. I could not believe it worked, and the really funny part is that several other children within earshot stopped and froze! I laughed out loud as I marched toward my daughter.

She was still about thirty feet away when I said, *"green light"*. I waited two seconds and quietly called out, *"red light"*.

Again she and several other kids did their best to stop on a dime.

When I caught her she looked up at me and anxiously awaited the next green light. After establishing that this was a walking green light, I said, quietly, *"green light,"* and we had a much better time in the mall.

This technique has worked and continues to work with her now that she is six and it also works for my three-year-old son. For example, it works for stopping them at the end of the driveway prior to running in the street. I thank my Father in heaven every time it works. I praise Him for teaching me such a valuable parenting tactic completely by accident. I do not have to be the big, mean mommy who won't let her kids run amuck, and I have on several occasions had people comment about how cute they are. Oh, there is one other benefit from this tactic—they cannot be loud or they will not hear the "light change."

God, as our Father and parent, needs us to be willing to stop and go when and where He says. He will stop us from danger and let us go into joy if we are able to hear the "light change." He knows the best for us. God as our teacher expects us to find ways to be gentle with our words, be creative and loving with the children that He has placed in our trust, and most importantly, we must teach them to listen for His voice.

Red light—stop and listen!

Green light—go make disciples of all you meet!

Jesus loves children because when someone says *go*, they *go*!!

Jesus loves you!

Wonderful Tales
Children Love Stories

Exodus 10:2

You will be able to tell wonderful stories to your children and grand-children about the marvelous things I am doing among the Egyptians to prove that I am Lord. (NIV)

Do your children love to read? I know that my children love to read and be read to and that their thirst for this is infinite. I never write "read to kids" at the top of my lengthy "to-do" list, but to my husband's chagrin, it often ends up taking priority over the rest of the list when I hear, "Mommy, weed to me! Weeeddd to meee!"

I always answer, "One book!" Yeah, right. Those times are so precious.

What kinds of stories do your children like to hear? How about adventure, gross, weird, funny, happily-ever-after, war and destitution, animal stories, heroes, villains, or beautiful poetry? How about Stephen King? Perhaps non-fiction or maybe those with fun messages about morals, values, and virtues are what your children are drawn to?

Let us look at that list from God's Word.

Adventure…How about David and Goliath, Lazarus, or the Israelites in the desert?

Gross and weird…Look in Ezekiel for the story about God's power to cause an entire army of dried bones to get up, grow skin, and start breathing.

Funny…Well, talking donkeys existed in Numbers 22:28 long before *Shrek* was ever a thought.

Happily-ever-after…The Israelites reach the Promised Land or the parts of Revelation that describe Jesus coming back for His church.

War and Destitution…Sodom and Gomorrah come quickly to mind.

Animal stories…There is Noah's ark or Jonah and the whale.

Heroes…Check out anyone in Hebrews 11, or just read the story of Jesus himself.

Villains…How about Satan, Judas, or Barrabas. By the way, they all lose in the end.

Stephen King-like…Revelation, if literally taken, beats all other stories ever told.

Perhaps you are more interested in non-fiction. Most kids like fiction because non-fiction is boring.

Well, do any of these stories sound boring to you?

Then there are the stories that convey a moral or virtuous message that we try to disguise as some cute book. Jesus taught the same moral truths in His parables. For example, the good Samaritan, the poor woman who gave her last two coins, and a host of others.

Well, it's all there…in the most amazing true story ever written.

What are some of your favorite Bible stories?

_____

_____

_____

_____

_____

_____

_____

I found myself wondering what my children would say was their favorite book. Would they say the Bible? Would it be one of the classic children's books? Take, for example, *Brown Bear, Brown Bear*. Do you know this book? My children love it. It is the first book that Kaylyn ever read to her brother, and Camper has it memorized. I love to rewrite things in reference to the Bible, so I thought we might rewrite *Brown Bear, Brown Bear*. Pick a category like "Characters from the Nativity" and try telling the story this way.

Jesus, Jesus what do you see? I see Mary looking at me!

Mary, Mary what do you see? I see Joseph looking at me!

Joseph, Joseph what do you see? I see a wise man looking at me….

I pray that we, as parents, can learn to help our children love God's Word. There is no greater adventure story in the world. I pray that each of our children come to know You, Father God, and be with You in victory when Jesus returns.

Can we be sure that our children will grow up to say that their favorite book is the Word of God? The only surefire way is to read it, make it fun, and love it ourselves. Children love to tell great stories. If they love it, they will share it, and if they share it, they can change the world.

Jesus loves children because they love stories. Jesus loves you.

WTW MOMENTS
WHO'S TEACHING WHOM?

WTW moments have occurred many times as my children have grown. I find myself in a situation where I am truly not sure who is teaching whom. I love these moments as a way of seeing the world through the eyes of Christ. I consider each of them an opportunity to practice humility and put my "know-it-all" pride aside. Our Father loves us enough to send us children who can and will put us in our place. Children demonstrate early in life the best way to approach things…they take small steps. He has also helped me see that children share freely and lovingly. They learn better, faster, and more than we can possibly imagine. Children will help. They know when home is the only reasonable place to be to find rest and peace. Children survive some pretty hard lessons and are persuadable. Children love gifts. As you read, take a moment to imagine a child at Christmas. They exude happiness and excitement. We can seek to be like Christ each day, and as we strive to grow in our faith, we, too, will beam with His light.

Baby Steps
Children Take Small Steps

2 Peter 1:5–8

For this very reason, make every effort to add to your faith goodness; and to goodness, knowledge; and to knowledge, self-control; and to self-control, perseverance; and to perseverance, godliness; and to godliness, brotherly kindness; and to brotherly kindness, love. For if you possess these qualities in increasing measure, they will keep you from being ineffective and unproductive in your knowledge of our Lord Jesus Christ. (NIV)

Remember when your children or grandchildren were first born? You found them to be a miracle, but they really did not do a whole lot. The only thing they produced was…well…Then things began to happen and the process of learning began.

1. We watched them struggle to push themselves up. How cute and how heavy was that great big head on that tiny body.
2. Then they accidentally rolled over for the first time. We did not always get to witness this event. We just knew that we did not put them to bed that way.
3. Next came sitting, and, boy, did we help that tiny body of mush try to learn some balance. It was a little like balancing a softball on a pile of play dough.
4. From there they figured out how to get from point A to point B. Some rolled, some got on all fours and sprawled, and some did the military creep.
5. One day they were able to sit themselves up and see that the world exists beyond six inches high.
6. Each skill built on the next…and they began to crawl proficiently.
7. They began pulling up on furniture and nearby legs.
8. They took tiny, tentative steps, usually attached to a loving hand from above.

9. Then those sweet babies took that first small step toward independence, followed by a teeter, and then a fall on a well padded diaper.
10. True independence for the child came when they became adept at the straight leg walk…when they could disappear from a room in the time it takes to take the phone off the hook!
11. Then came running, hopping, jumping, galloping, skipping, and the entire childhood motor skill repertoire.

In most cases this process occurs in a relatively commonsense sequence. God, our heavenly father, intends for our spiritual development to progress along the same lines, but the skills to accomplish are a little different.

Faith—is the initial pushing up stage where all we have is our acceptance of Jesus (regardless of where we come from).

Goodness—is the rollover and be slightly surprised stage: the emotional response to the newness of grace…and it is *good*!

Knowledge—is the early stages of intentional movement, where we learn the basics.

Self Control—is the realization that we can move on purpose, by choice, and that we can make our actions and words match our beliefs.

Perseverance—is the practice and improving stage, where we realize that although we do not want to sin, we must keep trying, do better, and continue to be forgiven.

Godliness—is the "I am on my Feet Stage"; I have the tools I need so what will God have me do with it?

Kindness—is the look-at-me-move stage, and look at all the opportunities! How can I share this wonderful new skill?

Love—is the ultimate stage of learning possibilities where we become the true "copy cat" of motion after walking, when we can love as Jesus did and see the world through Jesus' eyes. He is our role model for each new and wonderful skill we develop.

Take a moment and re-write <u>**2 Peter 1:5–7**</u> in first person. It becomes a powerful prayer

_____

_____

_____

_____

_____

_____

_____

Where are you in your faith? Are you in need of relearning from the beginning? Sometimes we don't realize that half the battle is holding our "big head" up. Jesus wants to come into our hearts and help us in this journey. We have to simply open the door.

What is one baby step that you could take this week?

_____

_____

_____

_____

_____

_____

_____

Jesus loves children because they take small steps. Jesus loves you!

Dandelion Principle
Children Share Freely

Acts 19:20

In this way the word of the Lord spread widely and grew in power.
(NIV)

I love to watch my son or daughter try to blow dandelion feathers. Sometimes they all come out at the same time and float away. Other times they will blow and only some of the feathers come out. Sometimes Camper just shakes it to death. No matter how they come off, believe me, they will all come off. As adults, we call them weeds; to children they are flowers that fly! What a difference in perspective. Let's look at God's Word like those dandelions. We can be adults and burn those dandelion seeds because they are only weeds. Or, when we are really out of touch, we spread weed seeds like those evil words, thoughts, and deeds that, when spread, only reap more weeds. That, my friend, is how we do Satan's work for him.

OR—We can be like children and blow the dandelion, and that one flower can multiply and grow many other "flowers that fly." We can be thrilled to share what we know. We can spread the Word of God as the miracle that it is and be thrilled every time a good wind blows those seeds really far. We can spread it and not be content until every last seed has been given the opportunity to fly. We can do as it says in Acts.

There are several parables about seeds in the New Testament. A few that we should recall are the parables of weeds, mustard seeds, the sower, and many more about bearing fruit. Dandelions are, in fact, "weeds" but how we look at them can serve as a reminder.

Before I speak…I need to ask myself, "Weed? Flower? Fruit?"

Weeds are of Satan, and I do not want to make his job easier.

Flowers (and dandelions) are pretty and may or may not serve a lasting purpose.

Fruit represents the result of careful planting and nurturing of those eternal seeds.

Take a moment and describe some times when you have been sowing either weeds, flowers, or fruit.

_____

_____

_____

_____

_____

_____

_____

We must share both flowers and fruit! Do God's work. Do it freely and do it with the joy of a child.

HINT: You have seen and will see "LJPPKGFGSc" throughout this book. Those letters represent the Fruits of the Spirit in Galatians 5:22-23.

Jesus loves children because they share freely. Jesus loves you.

"Guess What I Learned?"
Children Learn

Acts 13:49

The word of the Lord spread through the whole region. (NIV)

Do you yearn for the days of hearing the excitement in the voices of children when they learn something new? Early in school children love to tell what they do and what they learn. They tell everyone and we call every relative we can to share an amazing story of great intelligence with our families.

Do you remember potty training? Oh, the joy and public embarrassment of having a child announce to everyone that they need to go potty. My precious son wanted to show everyone when he went potty and would proudly proclaim his "poo-pee" accomplishment to everyone in the restaurant. Remember those first words, tying shoes, reading a word, taking off clothes, flushing the potty, feeding themselves, opening the refrigerator, dressing themselves, cleaning up a mess, putting on make-up at two years, discovering a new way to play with a toy, and the word "look." Each of these events, and many more, represent a stage in life when learning is what life is all about. It is a time when sharing what we learn—good, bad, or otherwise—is what makes life worth living.

My daughter was a very verbal toddler and we laughed a great deal because of her amazing ability to use language. When she was not quite two years old, she was in the living room playing with her blocks. She looked a little distressed, when she looked up and said, "Mommy, I fus-ter-ated! Theez blocks are not cop-er-ating!"

Needless to say, we had to leave the room so that we could laugh ourselves to tears. She was quickly learning language and was using it well.

On another occasion, just after her second birthday, she was in Mimi's kitchen; she opened two cabinet doors, stepped toward the cabinet between the two open doors, turned around, pulled the two doors so that they met at a point, and called out "Look Mimi, I'm in a triangle!"

We pretty much just stood there, mouths agape, and finally Mimi confirmed for my little geometry genius that she was right.

Children learn it, and then they share it. It really is not a difficult concept, and yet, we find it hard to share the greatest story ever told. How can we possibly lose our enthusiasm? The good news about Jesus is our only hope for eternity and guess what…if we spend our time sharing the good news, we do not have time to gossip or bear false witness, now do we?

Have you ever missed an opportunity to share with someone? Describe it and what you might do differently next time.

_____

_____

_____

_____

_____

_____

_____

Do you know of someone who needs to know Jesus' love? Do you need to know Jesus? He knows you and wants to have a relationship with you. He wants to be a part of your life, but you do have to confess your sin, which put Him on that cross, and then welcome Him into your heart. It really is just that simple!

_____

_____

_____

_____

_____

_____

_____

Jesus loves children because they learn. Jesus loves you.

"Ina Hewlp Eewe"
Children Help

Psalm 46:1

God is our refuge and our strength, an ever present help in trouble.
(NIV)

Recall for a moment the days when your toddlers actually wanted to help you with the chores around the house. They loved vacuuming, dusting, dishes, cleaning the bathroom counter, sweeping the floor, and so on. All those things they would soon complain about but at that point they thought were neat and interesting. There have been times when I was in a hurry, and their help created more of a problem by making us late, making a bigger mess, or making more work for me later. There have been major battles between my son and daughter to "be helpful" by opening the garage door or feeding the dog, and the stress that ensues from the screaming match usually outweighs the benefits of their "help." There have been times when I knew I could do it faster, better, and more efficiently, but because it was cute, and I wanted to encourage helpful behavior, I allowed them to help in spite of the sometimes inconvenient consequences.

Camper was two-and-a-half years old and I was putting the dishes in the dishwasher. When I grabbed the detergent he said, "Ina hewlp eewe!" It was not a suggestion. He and his little puckered mouth and furrowed brow were going to have a hand in pouring the powder into the trays. This was one of those cute times when we were not in a hurry and I could just encourage him and thank him for being helpful. We closed the door together, and he closed the handle and pushed the button to turn it on.

As he pushed the button I wondered how many times I had insisted on helping God, my Father, as he was cleaning up a mess that I had made. How many times have I created more of a problem for him by doing it my way or fighting about it? How many times had he groaned at my feeble efforts but with love and patience indulged me? Many of us have felt, at times, that God is not helping us or that He has abandoned us. Perhaps we were just too busy doing it our way. Perhaps He is waiting with great patience and encouragement for me, His child, to "help" things along only to have me create more of mess. He lovingly guides our hands and allows us to break the glass we were only holding with one hand. He allows us to close the door of the dishwasher just as the bottom rack is crashing into the back wall. He holds onto us with His strong hand as we push the correct button hoping that we will learn to clean up after ourselves. As He encourages us He is more than glad to help us.

Describe an experience when you thought for the moment that God had abandoned you.

_____

_____

_____

_____

_____

_____

_____

After that experience, what contributions did you probably make to that situation that perhaps interfered with God's ability to handle it better?

_____

_____

_____

_____

_____

_____

_____

Jesus loves children because they help. Jesus loves you.

"I Wanna Go Home"
Children Know Home

<u>Luke 2:47–50</u>

Everyone who heard him was amazed at his understanding and his answers. When his parents saw him, they were astonished. His mother said to him, "Son, why have you treated us like this? Your father and I have been anxiously searching for you." "Why were you searching for me?" he asked. "Didn't you know I had to be in my Father's house?" But they did not understand what he was saying to them. (NIV)

Children have a homing instinct that is unmatched on this earth. I don't mean they have a sense of direction but more of a sense of the right place to be. When my children are away from home and grow tired of whatever we are doing, the first whine is usually, "I waannnaaa goooo hooomme!" Home is safe. Home is family. Home is usually constant. Home is our place of rest, reassurance, and refuge. Home is where we are destined to be. We eat, sleep, play, grow, and develop at home.

Richard, my father-in-law, was on his deathbed. It had been a miserable couple of years. He was suffering and sleep deprived. He was battling demons we could not even begin to imagine. He was tired and sick. He could not breathe. He had been in ICU for over a month. He had been in and out of coherence, when one day he came to a very abrupt peace about going home to his heavenly Father. He, with Pastor Stephen's help, came to peace with his faith, his life, and his mistakes. As miserable as things had been, nothing could compare to the indescribable peace on his face when he knew he was finally going home, for good. I can only praise God for His mercy and power in that situation as I watched a man, whom we loved very much, go from completely tormented to having peace beyond understanding. As we watched him breathe his last breath we knew, without a doubt, that he was home.

My nephew, Michael, predicted his early death when he told his parents that, "It is time for me to go take care of Lindsay" (his sister who was born prematurely and passed away). He knew, and he, too, seemed to be at peace. He did pass away at the age of nine from injuries caused by a horrific car-semi-truck accident.

<u>Revelation 21:3–4</u> describes our heavenly home. Check it out and describe some of the most beautiful characteristics of that home.

_____

_____

_____

_____

_____

_____

There are some really beautiful, wonderful people who are there waiting for me in heaven. I love knowing that Jesus has prepared a place for me. A home, a heavenly home that words cannot describe, but so many come to peace when they know they are on their way home!

Think and reflect for a moment on the following questions. Is my home a place of peace? Is my home a place where my family can take refuge from the world? Is my home a place where my Father in heaven is welcome at any time to come and abide with us?

_____

_____

_____

_____

_____

_____

There are children today who have no home, which, for me, means they have no peace. There are children who live in homes where Christ is a curse word and nothing more. There are children who reside in homes that are not safe and are not places of refuge. I pray for those children that they might stumble into a church family that will teach them that there is no comfort like the comfort we can find in our Father's house.

Jesus asked his parents, "Did you not know you would find me in my Father's house?" How completely amazing! As a church, are we reaching out to the point that all are welcome? Jesus sought refuge in His Father's house…a house that cannot be destroyed or taken away because it is within us!

Jesus loves children because they know home. Jesus loves you!

Let Them Learn the Hard Way
Children Survive Hard Lessons

Deuteronomy 24:16

Fathers shall not be put to death for their children, nor children put to death for their fathers, each is to die for his own sin. (NIV)

Sydnie was nine months old at the time. She was pulling up on everything and taking several small steps at a time. She was in my living room, where I had just set up a TV tray before returning to the kitchen, where the rest of the adults were. All of a sudden we heard the blood-curdling scream of my tiny little niece. She had, of course, pulled up on the TV tray, and it fell on her. My dad was the first on the scene. He scooped her up. She had obviously taken two pretty nasty knocks over her left eye. She cried for several minutes and sought the comfort of familiar faces. Fortunately, she escaped the nasty bruises I thought she would develop. I am not sure if she learned any lesson about TV trays, but it happened and we all felt horrible.

Sometimes we find as parents that we just have to let them learn lessons the hard way. We desperately try to protect our children from any harm or danger. We try to teach our young children that climbing up a book shelf could have disastrous results, that playing with a scorpion hurts, and many other valuable "Don't touch the curling iron" lessons. As they grow, we seek to protect them from the emotional pain that comes with growing up and becoming a teenager. Parents all over the world would trade places with their children when they are suffering.

Our eternal salvation depends on our consciously choosing Christ. Many people are still "learning the hard way" when it comes to their relationship with God in heaven. The problem is that waiting too long or going into death having never learned or understood can result in spending eternity suffering in hell. We, as parents, cannot pay for our children's sins, we cannot justify their sins, and we cannot trade places with them in eternity, so we must teach, love, and guide them *now*. We must let them see Jesus in us. The bumps, bruises, and burns that our children receive from childhood lessons are nothing compared to an eternity apart from our Father.

Loving Father,

Help me survive the hard lessons in my life. Show me when I am responsible for them, and build in my heart and mind a desire to listen to Your voice and wisdom. Help me teach my children that actions have consequences and that we are each responsible for the choices we make.

In Jesus' Name,

Me

Jesus loves children because they survive hard lessons. Jesus loves you.

"Mommy, Santa, Jesus, *Hmmm*?"
Children Are Persuadable

Matthew 7:11

If you, then, though you are evil, know how to give good gifts to your children, how much more will your Father in heaven give good gifts to those who ask him! (NIV)

"Be Alert" was the title of Stephen's sermon that day and it was based on Luke 21:34-36. Be ready for Jesus to return. He was semi-reprimanding us to remember the true meaning of Christmas. He posed the question:

What are we focused on this time of year?

My list began somewhat as follows:

Christmas cards, parties, performances at church and at school, presents for everyone, canned food drives, my children and their desires, what to get everyone, preparing my home for guests, money, and so on. I really look forward to this time of year but not for the reasons most of you would think. Sure, I knew Jesus was the reason for the season, but let me tell you, at that time I had a five-year-old and a two-year-old at home, and the harsh reality was that my house often looked something like the following.

It was a Saturday morning around the first of December (just after that sermon on Luke 21:34–36). My children were watching cartoons; I was actually cleaning up the kitchen and trying to get some laundry done. I looked out into the living room, and I asked Kaylyn to take her shoes to her room. I heard "But mooommmmm," with that all-too-familiar whine, and she continued, "I wanna watch this!" I spun around, one eyebrow raised and I was instantly ready to combust…

When what to my wandering eye does appear?
A Rapunzal Barbie that's brand new this year.
She glances upon it and starts in to say
"I'll do it if you buy me this today!"
Then I, in my infinite wisdom, do cheer
"Get going or I will have Santa skip here!"
"NOOOO screams the siren as off she does go
With shoes and a toy she runs to and fro.
"It worked!" "She did it!" with one tiny threat,
A month of cooperation will now be no sweat!"

POOF—in pops Pastor Stephen's voice…as if I need another mother! Be Alert!…Yeah!…Okay! What if my heavenly Father parented like that? What if God looked at me and said, "Angela Lyn, if you don't cooperate right now I will not let Jesus bring you your gift! You remember, that grace and mercy all wrapped in blood, on a cross, given so that you can spend eternity in heaven."

What if my Lord returns and my children, who are a perfect gift in themselves, have grown up and they are more worried about pleasing Santa then God their Father in heaven? It would be tragic and embarrassing to be at the feet of my Lord trying to explain that. Take a minute and write what your children might say to Jesus right now.

_____

_____

_____

_____

_____

_____

_____

I will meet Jesus one day, I will do better focusing on the Christ part of Christmas, and I will do it year-round so that when He returns, I and my family will be ready.

Precious Father,

Help my children learn to discern. Place in me a strong ability to help them base their decisions on You. When I have parenting moments that are not making You proud, please convict my heart immediately. Thank you for the impressionable nature of children, but protect them and lead them away from temptation. Help me grow and become more faithful in my journey with You. Persuade my head that my heart is right, for inside my heart is where I want You to abide.

In Jesus' Name,

Me

Jesus loves children because they are persuadable. Jesus loves you.

Red Ribbon Gift
Children Love Gifts

John 3:16

For God so loved the world that he gave his one and only Son, that whoever believes in him shall not perish but have eternal life. (NIV)

Have you ever met a child who did not want to open a present? Maybe they said, "No mommy, it is pretty just like that. I think I will put it on my dresser and look at it. I will admire it and appreciate it for its simple beauty. I do not want to know what is in it, and I really do not need anything new, okay?"

Well, that has never happened in my house. My children are truly tortured by an unopened gift. If we put out Christmas presents early or they find a birthday gift somewhere, they are absolutely annoying until the day of opening. "Mommy, can I open just one?" "How 'bout I open one for being so good?" "Mommy can I open one if I clean my room?" My personal favorite was when Kaylyn came home from kindergarten and said, "Mommy, I really want you to open your present now!" She then waited for effect. "But, if you open yours, I get to open one of mine!" (sly little smile).

I believe God wants us to look at the gift of Jesus Christ in exactly that way. There He waits, wrapped in red; waiting for us to accept the gift. What do we find when we open it? After breaking through the red ribbon (his blood sacrifice), we find the package is perfectly white (His purity), and we tear through the paper to see what is inside. Inside we find grace, mercy, and forgiveness, and we find that we are now clean. By accepting this precious gift, we are opening our hearts to Christ. We accept what is inside—free, perfect, and awesome. We are saying, "Yes! I love Him. I want Him in my heart. I want Him to be my friend forever. I love Him! Thank you, Father!"

Once we open that gift, our lives can never be the same again. May any red ribbon remind us of the most amazing gift ever given.

John 3:16 (re-written for our children)

For we love our children so much that we give them wonderfully awesome gifts; so that whosoever opens the package shall not be unhappy, but have a wonderful, but perishable, reminder of us. Let's remember to give them Jesus, the everlasting gift from a Father who loves them more than we ever could.

I want you to first write your name in the blank space below and then write the names of your loved ones.

John 3:16

For God so loved (_____

_____

_____

_____

_____)

that he gave his one and only Son, that whoever believes in him shall not perish but have eternal life.

Jesus loves children because they love gifts. Jesus loves you.

911 Parenting Moments

Finally we will venture into the realm of parenting that we hope to someday experience in heaven. God is a loving and wonderful Father and in His arms we can find peace. We can, even after having been away, learn that we too are childlike in our relationship with Him. Our instincts tell us that He is our sanctuary. We run to Him in our times of trouble and when we seek Him He is there. It is OK for us to need and want God's protection but when we give with all our heart He will bless us beyond measure. There is a saying, "You cannot out give God!" Take heart, be persistent, and listen for His voice. It is these promises from God's Word, and the very real experiences that we have with our children, that will allow us to see God as The Ultimate Father!

"But I Can Make It Fit!"
Children Understand *Peace*

Isaiah 11:6–8

The wolf will live with the lamb, the leopard will lie down with the goat, the calf and the lion and the yearling together; and a little child will lead them. The cow will feed with the bear, their young will lie down together, and the lion will eat straw like the ox. The infant will play near the hole of the cobra, and the young child put his hand into the viper's nest. (NIV)

In this scripture we can relate to a peace that is incomprehensible to us now. We see dangerous, ferocious animals lying down with their enemies. We have a picture painted for us that describes a child in the middle of that amazing image of peace. It is written that a child will lead them. That is very humbling to me…a child, not a big, all-knowing, strong, wonderfully prepared adult. Children seem to be fascinated with what adults would consider dangerous things. Children will gravitate toward a light socket or a scorpion on the floor. Children, in their innocence, will see a strange animal and gleefully say, "Doggie!" I recall my nine-month-old son crawling over to a scorpion. When he reached for it, the scorpion stung him. He cried in anguish as his hand swelled to nearly twice its normal size.

As I reflect on this now, I understand that children cannot even begin to fathom that there is anything on this wonderful planet that might harm them. They do not know fear. They know and expect peace. Adam and Eve had no need to be fearful because God was with them in the garden. That peace that children expect, and that Adam and Eve experienced, was perfect. True peace is innocent. It is faithful and it is right in the grand scheme of God's original design. But we live in a world where dogs do bite, scorpions do sting, ant mounds can hurt, stoves and curling irons are hot, and electrical sockets (which we put at eye level to a two-year-old) are not simply a puzzle with a missing piece (be it a pencil, a toy, or whatever). The garden was perfect. Heaven will be perfect, and this scripture in Isaiah grasps what children innately know.

We have created a world that needs to be feared. Satan has caused great turmoil, and we are forced to raise our children to learn that not everything or everyone is nice.

What are some things that we can do in our daily walk to make our world a little more peaceful?

_____

_____

_____

_____

_____

_____

_____

We need to remember that forcing something into a light socket will give us a shock.

It says a little child will lead them. We can't lead if we are afraid. Remember that!

Jesus loves children because they understand _peace_. Jesus loves you!

Don't Stop Them
Children Have Great Instincts

Matthew 19:14

Jesus said, "Let the little children come to me, and do not hinder them, for the kingdom of heaven belongs to such as these." (NIV)

My five-year-old daughter was sitting next to me in church when she leaned over to tell me that when she went up for children's church the children were going to sing.

I asked, "You are going to sing?"

She replied simply, "Yeah."

I was skeptical because of an episode that had resulted in us vowing to never force our daughter to participate in any musical event again. Two weeks prior to this day she had decided that she was shy and did not want to sing in church with the other children. This is a child who had been singing every word from her mouth for the past five years! We made her go to the front of the church with the other Sunday school kids who were scheduled to sing. She proceeded to make the ugliest face ever on a five-year-old, pout, stomp her foot, and not sing one word to a song she sings constantly! It was one of those moments when I, as a parent, wanted to match her scene with a hair yankin' spankin' right out the back of the church, where the real punishment would begin. I was livid for an array of reasons that don't really matter, but she did not go to children's church to play that day.

Anyway, back to the positive story...I was thrilled and shocked that she was going to sing. When they finally called for the children she nearly sprinted to the front of the church, maneuvered her way to the front of the group, and proceeded to sing with all her might. She was showing her tonsils with that open angel mouth, and she sang each word as if it were the most important message ever told. We sat in our pew, smiling...no chuckling, when I noticed several people were looking back at Rick and me, chuckling themselves. She had no inhibitions, she was not embarrassed, and she sang as if Jesus were sitting in the back row.

When has one of your children embarrassed you? Take a minute and recall the situation.

_____

_____

_____

_____

_____

_____

_____

Has your child ever made you so proud you just might burst? Write about it.

_____

_____

_____

_____

_____

_____

What a difference! To this day I do not know what caused the change in attitude. When Jesus said, "the kingdom of heaven belongs to such as these," I now have a very vivid image of my beautiful five-year-old singing with every ounce of her being to our Lord and Savior. When we sing, do we sing like children, who sing because it is fun? Do we sing for an audience that consists only of Jesus Christ? We learn inhibitions. We learn to be ashamed. We learn fear. Children are beautiful, fearless, and shameless. Perhaps that is why Jesus said, "let them come to me." Perhaps He knew they were not ashamed to love Him!

Are you able to show your love for Jesus to those you love most? Why or why not?

_____

_____

_____

_____

_____

_____

Are your "instincts" to hide your faith? Children know Jesus. Do you? Do you want to? He knows everything about me and still loves me. I want to know everything about Him because I love Him. I can say that knowing Him has made my "instincts" better.

Jesus loves children because they have great instincts. Jesus loves you.

"Mommy, I'm Scared"
Children Come Running

Isaiah 41:10

So do not fear, for I am with you; do not be dismayed, for I am your God. I will strengthen you and help you; I will uphold you with my righteous right hand. (NIV)

What are your children afraid of? Camper is afraid of sounds on the window, shadows, and monsters. We deal with each fear as it comes, and we know that he will outgrow most of them. I do, however, recall a time when Kaylyn became fearful and I could not do a thing to comfort her.

She was four-and-a-half years old and was very sick. She had a high fever, which for her was not uncommon, and I waited for two days, to no avail, for the fever to subside. I finally told her I was going to have to take her to the doctor. She was very lethargic but began expressing her fears. "Will I have to have a shot?"

At that moment I made one of the biggest mistakes of my life, when I said, "No, honey, they will check you out and probably give you a chewy antibiotic to get rid of the bug in your lungs."

We got to the doctor and he immediately ordered an x-ray. She was showing signs of RSV and pneumonia. I was holding a very sick little girl in my arms, who was now becoming very scared. He was talking about the hospital, when he said those fateful words, "She will have to have a shot."

She began to cry her eyes out, and I was not much better. I had just unknowingly lied (mommy fear #1) to my four-year-old, and now I was in the precarious position of consoling her while she anticipated, for what seemed like an eternity, the shot (child fear #1). Of course this was no joke of a shot. This one was going to make her thigh hurt for a couple of days (mommy fear #2), and I had to hold her down to allow the nurse to do this to her (mommy fear #3). She has forgiven me (mommy fear #4), and I have learned a very valuable and painful lesson about the unconditional trust my children have in my word. I held her, unable to really console her, but once it was over I could comfort her in her time of pain. God's Word is far more trustworthy, and I need to be teaching my child that there are many things on this earth that are mean, are scary, and cannot be trusted. A Veggie-Tales song is entitled, *God Is Bigger than the Boogie Man*, which teaches that God is always with us and He is bigger than all of our fears.

Do you have any irrational fears? I have a completely irrational fear of spiders. It is ridiculous enough that a spider once kept me out of my house. We can ask God to help us with those fears. Surrender them now.

_____

_____

_____

_____

_____

_____

The flip side of the coin is the type of fear that results in and from respect. We want children to fear or respect the consequences to some actions. You run into the street, you could get squished by a car (mommy fear); you wander from mommy, you might get lost (mommy fear); you talk to strangers, you could get kidnapped or hurt (mommy's greatest fear); you break the rules, you will be punished (kid fear).

Deuteronomy 31:11–12

You must read this law to all the people of Israel…Do this so that your children who have not known these laws will hear them and will learn to fear the Lord your God. (NIV)

Are we teaching our children the same fear or respect for God's laws? There is a great deal of evidence in the Bible that supports our Father's stern hand to disobedient peoples! Do my children fear me more than they fear the consequence of an eternity in hell? Have I taught my children that together we will seek to please God by following the example of Jesus, or are my children more worried about Mommy getting mad?

What do you think?

_____

_____

_____

_____

_____

_____

The shot was awful, but the consequences without it were gravely worse. It was an instance of weighing my options. Sometimes parenting means making decisions for our children that are immediately painful but necessary for the long term. Are there experiences in our lives that may fall into that category…immediately painful, but entirely necessary to bring us running back to our Father, so that we can be with Him for eternity?

_____

_____

_____

_____

_____

_____

_____

Father,

Thank you for upholding us and strengthening us. Help us discern the difference between irrational fear that holds us captive, and the fear of the Lord, which sets us free. I love You and know in my head that I have nothing to fear when You are with me. Help me know when my brain and my irrational fears are getting the best of me.

In Jesus' Name,

ME

Jesus loves children because they come running. Jesus loves you. Run to *Him*!

"Mommy, Where Are You?"
Children Seek Until They Find

Proverbs 8:17

I love those who love me, and those who seek me find me. (NIV)

I heard my son calling for me. He was searching through the house. "Mommy, where are you?" There was a tad more desperation with each call. When he finally found me in the kitchen he asked, "Where you go?"

I chuckled and then realized the kitchen was the last place he looked and apparently could not figure out how or why I would be there. Major Proverbs 31 failure! ("A wife of noble character who can find?…She gets up while it is still dark; she provides food for her family." Verses 10, 15.) OK, so I do not spend much time in the kitchen. The second part of that realization was that he actually was concerned, and when he could not find me immediately, it crossed his mind that I might have actually left.

What then, is it like for us? Is God quietly waiting for us in some area of our life where we don't expect to see Him? I am finding my Father in strange places much more frequently these days. I see Him in a person or behind a door that is opening or closing in front of me. I see Him in a sick friend whose faith has not wavered. I have seen Him in a sweet young lady with cerebral palsy who, on a daily basis, blesses the people around her. I have found my Father waiting patiently for a lost child to come home. I have seen Him in tears and in laughter. I see Him in my children almost every day. I watch Him work in the lives of my family. He is everywhere!

He also never, ever, leaves me. I often call out to Him, usually for reassurance that He is there. Sometimes I get a little more desperate and, like Camper, call out with heightened concern. "Father, where are you? Where are you?"

Then it dawns on me…I could have called out to my son Camper. I could have sought him out, but there I stood, waiting for him to come to me. I waited for him to find me so that I could scoop him up and say, "I was right here all along," and then smile as I hugged my sweet child. Suppose our Father in heaven is also waiting for us to come to Him. He is waiting for us to find Him so that He can scoop us up and say, "I was right here all along," and then smile and hug us, His sweet children.

What is it that you seek most in your life?

_____
_____
_____
_____
_____
_____
_____

As you reread what you wrote are there some things that a really loving Father would love to help you find? Ask Him! Seek Him! Find Him!

Jesus loves children because they seek until they find. Jesus loves you.

"Oh Mr. Toad…Why Did You Hop into the Road?"
Children Need Protection

Isaiah 8:11

The LORD spoke to me with his strong hand upon me, warning me not to follow the way of this people. (NIV)

Kaylyn was five and we were in the front yard while getting ready to go somewhere. My husband's truck was parked on the street and she walked out in front of it to get to her side of the truck to get in. I screamed her name and scared her more than half to death. After jumping out of her skin, she turned to me in her mini-adult voice and calmly said, "Mommy, why did you yell at me?" and her eyes filled with tears.

There are times as a parent when we just react. I do not know any parent who will not yank the arm off of a toddler to prevent him or her from walking into the street when traffic is coming. I am sure that maybe you can rationalize with your excited two-year-old or forgetful five-year-old, but I have not found that bending down saying, in my calm, slightly patronizing voice, "Now, honey, if you run out into the street you could get squished and it might hurt a little so please do not do that again…okeedokee?" works quite well enough.

Kaylyn learned a silly song about crossing the street when she was in preschool. The song is as follows and is sung to the tune of *Oh, Christmas Tree*.

Oh, Mr. Toad, Oh, Mr. Toad…Why did you hop into the road?
Oh, Mr. Toad, Oh, Mr. Toad…Why did you hop into the road?
You were so green and really fat…Now you're brown and really flat
Oh, Mr. Toad, Oh, Mr. Toad…Why did you hop into the road?

She knows it. She understands it, but a cute song never prevented her from darting into the street. So how does our Father feel when He sees us heading into a dangerous street? I imagine there are times when He is standing in the driveway cautioning me to stop, look, listen, wait, and proceed slowly. There are many other times when He is yelling at me to stop and go a different way. He even reaches out and yanks me back. I look up and cry at the pain I am experiencing, and He waits for me to figure out where I went wrong. How many times do I push God to the point of yanking me back to himself? He loves me…He loves you, and He, under no circumstance, will let me run into danger that could permanently separate me from Him. Describe a situation where God "yanked" you in another direction. It often looks and feels like a door slamming in your face!

_____

_____

_____

_____

_____

_____

_____

Reread **Isaiah 8:11** and know beyond a shadow of a doubt that God is a parent just like you who will do anything to keep you from the dangers of this world, which are here because of our sin.

Jesus loves children because they need protection. Jesus loves you.

Tooth Fairy Forgot to Get Change
Children Give Wholeheartedly

Mark 12:43–44

Calling his disciples to him, Jesus said, "I tell you the truth, this poor widow has put more into the treasury than all the others. They all gave out of their wealth; but she, out of her poverty, put in everything—all she had to live on." (NIV)

When Kaylyn lost her second tooth, shortly after her fifth birthday, apparently the tooth fairy forgot to get change because she left a $5.00 bill. This caused great trepidation for Daddy, Mimi, Grandma, and many other family members, but that $5.00 would soon result in a valuable lesson. On Sunday morning Kaylyn got herself dressed and came from her room announcing that she wanted to give that money to church.

I actually thought, and started to say, no because she usually gives only $1.00 in church. God immediately interrupted my thoughts with, "Why not let her give it? What is she going to buy with that $5.00 that you would not willingly provide for her?" She wanted to give her own money and I was about to stop her...I must be an idiot! "Satan, get out of my head!" So I actually said, "Honey, that is a wonderful idea! That is a lot of money that can really help our church. You, my precious angel, have made Jesus very happy right now, and I am very proud of you!"

God, my Father, is the exact same way. God gives us our daily bread; the Bible commands us to tithe 10% from the first fruits—because it belongs to Him anyway. So why do we hesitate? A child, my child, taught me that giving is only giving when we give it all. Giving just what we can afford does not demonstrate faith in our Father, who will lovingly and willingly give us the desires of our heart. The widow could have chosen to give one coin, but she chose to give two—her last two—coins!

How can we become more like the widow in this scripture?

_____

_____

_____

_____

_____

_____

_____

Jesus loves children because they give wholeheartedly. Jesus loves you!

Tune-Out Technique
Children Fervently Persist

1 John 5:14

This is the confidence we have in approaching God: that if we ask any-thing according to his will, he hears us. (NIV)

I was standing in my mother's kitchen talking with her. My brain was working slightly slower than usual. My two-year-old daughter was talking, but I was hearing, "wa-wa…waawaaawaaaa…mommmmmmmiiiiieeeee!"

"WHAAATTT!" I respond loud and irritated.

She looked horrified and temporarily could not remember what she wanted. "Mommy, may I have a chip?"

These were the realizations that came in that instance.

1. Vocal sounds from the floor get to my ears but not to my brain.
2. I am very skilled at "tuning out" my daughter (this is not good).
3. Had I at least acknowledged her, I could have prevented both of our high volume outbursts.

As a mother, I have spent a great deal of time trying to figure out how to train my children to not interrupt while I am on the phone. Other than a raised eyebrow and a "Wait!" pointer finger, I have not figured it out yet. The phone ringing is apparently directly linked to the volume, intensity, and quantity of demands from my children. Ignoring them also has the same correlation. Kaylyn is now five-and-a-half and my son is two-and-a-half and I am very skilled at "tuning out" both children. I can "tune out" whining, crying, tattling, yelling at each other, and even just basic requests. Over the last year, with two tiny voices to be heard, I have also learned that my husband has absolutely no "tune out" ability. I can "tune out" for several minutes, and then in walks Daddy from the outside. It infuriates him when the kids are whining and I have apparently been ignoring them for who knows how long. I know in those moments that he feels like we have installed chalkboards all over our house for the sole purpose of scraping our fingernails against them. I don't mean to do that to him, but it does usually stop when Daddy walks in. Thanks, Honey! Sometimes we feel like God is tuning us out, but our Father in heaven, like my husband, does not have the ability to "tune out." I have realized that I can be a great whiner, yeller, tattler, crier, and asker. God hears and knows all. He loves me and oftentimes I forget that He always acknowledges me. He says things such as, "Just a minute," "Be patient, my child," "I heard you, but that is not such a good idea," "Yes, my child," and sometimes He says, "I said *no!*"

Think for a moment about a time or an event that felt like a "No!" Looking back at it now, can you find the blessing?

_____

_____

_____

_____

_____

_____

_____

Jesus loves children because they fervently persist. Jesus loves you.

You Thought They Weren't Listening Children Listen

Matthew 26: 28

This is my blood of the new covenant, which is poured out for many for the forgiveness of sins. (NIV)

We are sitting in church and Pastor Stephen is about three or four minutes into his sermon. Kaylyn is diligently working on her children's coloring page. I am taking notes. Rick and his mom are listening intently as Stephen captivates us with his sermon. He then says, "We are made clean because we have been washed in the blood of the lamb."

Kaylyn pipes up, "Mommy, that is yucky, do we really have to take a bath in blood?" She is absolutely mortified.

We are chuckling to the point of shaking the pew and looking at each other not sure exactly how to respond. I lean over to tell her, "Not exactly, honey, we can talk after church."

It takes the remainder of the sermon for us to compose ourselves. The service continues and Stephen begins the communion liturgy. At this point he says, "This is my blood shed for you." Now we assume that our children do not pay much attention to any one particular thing, but Kaylyn says, louder this time, "Eeeeuuuuu, Mommy are we really going to drink blood, I don't want to!"

The pew is now shaking again, and we tell her, "Honey, it is not blood."

Keep in mind that she is only three, and so much information creates overload analysis in her tiny brain. We can barely keep it together, and all I can picture is Kaylyn going back to preschool and telling her teacher that in our church we bathe in and drink blood!

Several years have passed and Kaylyn is coming closer to an understanding of communion and the sacrifice that Jesus made that is the "free bath" by which we are made clean.

Children are amazing listeners when you think they are not listening. This little tale should remind you that children are very literal in their understanding of this world. Many parents have embarrassing stories of when a child has repeated something that they said, something that maybe they desperately wish had never been said. Children are watching, listening, and copying our actions. Are our children seeing Christ-like actions in us? Are children learning…by any means necessary…that Jesus sacrificed His blood for each one of us, and that we may partake in the forgiveness of that sacrifice every time we sin?

Jesus loves children because they listen. Jesus loves you.

CLOSING THOUGHTS FROM THE MONKEY BARS

A friend of mine was once on a long trip with her family when suddenly her two-year-old daughter began having fever-induced seizures in the back seat of the car. Her husband sped toward the nearest hospital as my friend hopped into the back seat and began trying to comfort her baby. After helplessly holding her for about ten minutes of repeated seizures, she was terrified, crying, angry, and at the end of her rope, when she literally screamed, "Okay, God, if you want her, take her! She's yours!" The seizing stopped immediately, and her baby girl fell limp into her arms. She cried all the way to the hospital, thankful for the mercy, but it took that surrender for her to understand that God was in control and that her child was only entrusted to her. She did not own her.

I have another friend whose teenage son is torturing her with the bad decisions he is making right now. She is a Godly woman, but she has found herself at the end of her parental rope. In her anguish she clings to the promise in **Proverbs 22:6**, "Train a child in the way he should go, and when he is old he will not turn from it."

God provides us with very clear guidelines for perfect parenting in His Word. As we close *Monkey Bar Adventure*, I want to go back to our original list of characteristics that demonstrated the paradigm that we can only improve as Godly parents when we first seek to become perfect children of God. We all strive, usually under our own power, to be the ideal parent. We forget that God is our perfect example, and we don't always look at our children as He sees them. I want to reflect, for a moment, on a list of very perfect parents that are described in God's Word. They are perfect for one distinct reason, and I challenge you to discern that reason.

In **Genesis 22** we read of Abraham, who was willing, when God tested him, to sacrifice his son Isaac on the altar. Abraham is considered one of the great heroes of faith, and his family would exceed the numbers of stars in the heavens for his faithfulness. Moses' mother placed her precious baby in a basket in the river allowing the daughter of Pharaoh to find and raise Moses. Her faithfulness resulted in the freedom of the Israelites. Job, having lost all of his children and family, never wavered in his devotion to God. He did not like all that he had to endure nor did he understand why he had to endure it, but as a result of his faithfulness, God blessed him beyond all the fortune and family he could imagine.

Then there were the two prostitutes who stood before Solomon fighting over a baby. In <u>1 Kings 3:26</u> we read about Solomon commanding that the baby be cut in half. When the first woman spoke up saying, "Please, my Lord, give her the living baby! Don't kill him!" Solomon knew that only a mother could make that sacrifice. He declared her the mother and reunited her with her son.

Then we look into the heart and soul of Mary, the mother of Jesus, who knew that God had intimately and intentionally touched her life. She had to have cried and mourned as her baby was brutalized and crucified. Our Bible does not provide much insight into whether she wavered in faith or became angry, or if she questioned in anguish why this was happening…but she was willing to surrender her baby into the arms of God. We have the gentle picture of her standing with Jesus through it all and then holding his lifeless body when they took Him from the cross. Her faithfulness resulted in the salvation of all mankind.

Finally we have God, a Father who was willing to sacrifice His one and only Son for the likes of each of us. Jesus could have said, "Nope, I am not doing it! They don't care or deserve it!" Think for a moment how that would not only have changed history but how it would have changed our future. Not good! Instead Jesus called out to His Father and said, "Why have you forsaken me?" How utterly agonizing that must have been for God, the ultimate parent, to hear those words. Do you suppose He sat on the edge of His throne just dying to get up and rescue His son, perhaps just to prove that He had not forsaken his precious Jesus? God has heard the same heart-wrenching words that many parents hear and agonize over. We are not exempt from the pain that accompanies raising children. God knows and understands how hard it is to sacrifice and surrender your children. He understands what it feels like to watch a child suffer. God knows each of us, our needs, and our hopes.

At the end of our parenting rope, we will always find God, the perfect parent, willing to catch our children when we cannot. Surrender, not faithfulness, is the commonality in each of these biblical heroes and in these two friends whose very personal examples of sacrifice have forever touched my life. As we parent our children, God will help us and give us wisdom and courage, but we have to surrender them to Him, as hard as it is to believe that someone else can know better for our children. Love your children, give them your best, but remember our children are really our brothers and sisters in a family for which God is the ultimate and only parent. He is standing with us as we traverse the monkey bars of life, waiting at the other end to greet us and say, "Well done, good and faithful servant."

PRAYER FROM THE MONKEY BARS

Where there is a blank, please insert your name!

Precious Lord and Father,

I thank You for this journey and the opportunity to share what You have placed on my heart. You are an almighty God who loves us more than we can imagine. You graciously provide for our needs each day, and You have entrusted us with the awesome privilege and responsibility of raising children into a relationship with a parent who will never fail them. Lord, I pray that _____ will come to know the amazing power You have as a Father and friend.

To each reader, I pray that God will touch your heart and fill you with Christ-like character. I pray for you as you endeavor to build God's kingdom. I challenge you to go back to God's Word each day and seek His perfect parental guidance and spiritual strength. I believe in the power of God's Word. It is the one true instrument of teaching, correcting, rebuking, and encouraging that we have from our Father. As you go through scripture, take notes, rewrite it in first person, and claim the promise in that verse in the name of our redeemer, Jesus Christ! I claim the promises in His Word, which He so lovingly compiled, that we might grow closer to Him each time we open our Bibles. You, _____, are a precious Child of God, not by choice, but by grace. We are brothers and sisters in one heavenly family, conceived by our Father, saved by Jesus, and lead by the Spirit!

As we leave the Monkey Bar Adventure I pray that Father God will renew our commitment to the wonderful spiritual adventure that awaits each of us. Forgive us when we are monsters. Help us when we are monkeys, and encourage us when we are angels. Thank You for Your Word as a love letter of promise to each of us. Thank you for each child placed in our life that reminds us of You. Help us remember that when we strive to be a more faithful child of God, we can then and only then become a better parent.

In the Name of Grace,
LJPPKGFGSc,
Angela

ALPHABETICAL INDEX

Scripture quotations are taken from the
New International Version of the Bible.

WORKS CITED

The author would like to acknowledge to following sources and people for their contribution to *Monkey Bar Adventure*.

Sources cited in text

a. Katy McBeth—permission to use story granted on April 12, 2005

b. Josiah Leonard—permission to use e-mail
   Granted by Bull Leonard on March 29, 2005

c. Rubye Kelly—permission to use story granted on June 5,2005

d. Stephen Schmidt—Forward and permission to quote

e. I would like to thank the creator of BibleGateway.com
   © Copyright 1995-2005 <u>Gospel Communications International</u>.
   It has been and will continue to be a fantastic Biblical resource.

f. All Scripture quotations are taken from
   Holy Bible, New International Version © Copyright 1984
   Life Application Bible, New International Version © Copyright 1991
   Study Bible, New International Version © Copyright 1996

MINISTRY
FROM THE
MONKEY BARS

A multi-faceted ministry designed to encourage all of God's people. Our Father in heaven uses our own children to teach us valuable biblical lessons. Using scripture, drama, music, comedy, story-telling, object lessons, and real life examples, we will look at some common characteristics of children. We will learn how, through those funny and frustrating stories, we can begin to understand why Jesus continued to tell us that we must become like them to inherit the Kingdom of Heaven.

I look forward to meeting you in person and having the opportunity to share with you and your organization. If you are in need of encouragement, revitalization, and/or a spiritual lift, I hope you will consider allowing Ministry from the Monkey Bars to pay you a visit.

For more information on

Ministry from the Monkey Bars

Please feel free to call Angela Kirkpatrick at 254-518-6421 or e-mail angelakirkpatrick@hot.rr.com

978-0-595-35624-9
0-595-35624-9

Printed in the United States
37155LVS00007B/310-408